Vision in Action

Be empowered to achieve the success

you've dreamed of.

By: David March

First published by Dog Ear Publishing
4010 W. 86th Street, Ste H Indianapolis, IN 46268
www.dogearpublishing.net

ISBN: 978-1-4575-2660-2

This book is printed on acid-free paper.

Printed in the United States of America

<u>Dedication</u>

This book is dedicated to all who dare to believe in themselves as they travel life's journey, and to Mom, Yvette March. who never stopped believing in me. She clarified my concepts, spent endless hours giving her thoughts on revising and editing and supported me all the way through!

Acknowledgments

This book is a result of many minds and philosophies. I'm thankful for the inspiration and wisdom of these many thinkers, from the Far-East to the West. Their wisdom lives on and has not been forgotten

I thank God for the ability to synthesize the information I've gathered and the ability He's given me to write it down in this book.

I'm deeply grateful for the support, guidance, and patience of my parents as we went through many ups and downs, suggestions, and revisions.

I wish to thank my Editors, Frederick Doot for his devotion to the book and for the countless hours spent on drafts and revisions. I also wish to thank the editor of Dog Ear publishing for her comments and suggestions.

I wish to acknowledge the invaluable help of:

Contributing Editor, Thomas Hauck, for adding the section about Joe Ades

Creative Illustrators: James Art Ville and Eddie Egesi
Front Cover Design:
Frank O'Dowd, James Art Ville and Eddie Egesi

<u>Preface</u>

This book was created for several reasons. It will provide you with a comprehensive and objective view of the barriers in life that prevent you from achieving the success you deserve. It has its greatest application in personal growth, career counseling, personal, and professional leadership, work/life balance, and working effectively with others to get the most out of life. It is my hope that this book becomes a common text for understanding yourself in relation to the above areas so that you will be better prepared for life's challenges.

One of the reasons why I wrote this book is that I believe some of the same struggles I have had; others will have as well since we are all human. Like many, I searched for answers to life's questions such as Who am I? Where do I fit in? What career path should I follow? How do I accomplish my goals in the most effective way and where can I find guidance?

With a seeking spirit, I began doing research into finding answers to these questions; the product of my research is this book.

I integrated and emphasized the thinking and works of such notable writers as Joseph Campbell and Carl Jung, as well as success writers including Stephen J. Kraus, Steven Covey, and Malcom Gladwell. I also included spiritual teachings providing insights into the human experience, pulling from Buddhism, Taoism, Christianity, and different principles of the Institute for Professional Excellence in

Coaching (IPEC). Lastly, If you wish to read more about the research I have done over the years in books, film, scholarly articles and journals please refer to my bibliography.

Another reason is that I wanted to assist others in the discovery process of who they are and connect them with a satisfying career or guide them to achieving their vision in life. Throughout my high school and college years, I struggled to find solid answers to some of the questions I posed earlier. Many were too eager to steer me into pre-set pathways that did not celebrate my strengths or meet my interests and goals. Through my research and personal experience, I have come to understand that we are all unique and gifted in some special way. We just have to discover and believe it. From a general internet search, I discovered this quote attributed to Albert Einstein – "Everybody is a genius. But if you judge a fish by its ability to climb a tree, it will live its whole life believing that it is stupid."

I hope you enjoy this book!

<u>Introduction</u>

This book takes you on a journey to awaken the hero inside of you!

In it, I will teach you "The Hero's Journey" the 12 steps it goes through and how to activate the true human resource laying dormant inside of you.

I'll describe each step in-detail and the actions to take along the way to make the journey a successful one.

Let's go into detail about who is the hero.

The hero serves as an inspiring identity for others. The hero gives others hope. The hero shows us that despite his or her own shortcomings and obstacles, success is possible. As the hero's light shines, its aura inspires others around him.

In becoming this hero, you will seek to liberate and rescue yourself from the forces of despair and inertia. As the hero you should seek to stop being held down by oppressors, attempt to overcome personal depression and hopelessness. Through the hero's courage and determination he or she will show others that they are also capable of achieving greatness.

To re-emphasis this point consider this quote

"We are each the scriptwriter of our own triumphant drama. We are also its protagonists. In the same vain Shakespeare wrote "All the world's a stage / and all the men and women merely players"

This book and its chapters have been broken into the three main stages of *The Hero's Journey*,

- **Stage one** is described as *the preparation, the departure,* the beginning of *the separation from the ordinary world.* It covers chapters one – four. The topics of these chapters include **mind maps, mandalas, goals setting, the importance of listening, and partnerships.**

- **Stage two** is described as *the descent, initiation,* and *journey.* This stage talks about the understanding of the "self," your independence and identity, and your individual journey. Stage two corresponds to chapters five through eight in the book. In these chapters I deal with the concept of "revealing the authentic you." For this reason, it can also be called the soul journey. You will find the following topics discussed in these chapters: **A general theory of individuality, theory behind personality assessments, Applications of personality assessments,** and **Building up Engagement.**

- **Stage three** is described as *the return* and *re-integration to the ordinary world,* understanding your interdependence, becoming whole, and finally, completion. Once the journey is over the cycle begins again.

We have gone full circle and it's time for another circle. The end is a new beginning. This is covered in chapter nine. Its title is: "The Return."

What makes me uniquely qualified to be your guide along this journey?

well, I would say it is my determination to revitalize Carl Jung's and Joesph Campbell work and bring it into the

corporate world and it's my desire to disseminate the
understanding I have spent to date about $50,000 dollars on.
This is through personal development programs and books,
getting certified as a Certified Professional Coach from iPec,
one on one and group mentorship programs, tony robbins
workshops, Tai Chi Classes, leadership courses and general
life coaching and weekend re-treats.

This book is a collection of years of study and research on both
theoretical and practical experience, I have had when coaching
others and being coached myself. I have been investing in
personal growth for eight years now.

In Truth, there are many others that ARE more qualified than
me to talk about these concepts. There are people at the Joseph
Campbell foundation, there are legends of Analytical
Psychology like John Beebe. But simply put, they didn't.

The approach I have taken with this book comes from the
angle of transformation coaching and I have cited my sources
along the way.

Who is this book for and what problems does it solve.

This book is for Artists, Empaths, Entrepreneurs, CEO's
Directors, VPs, Disruptors, Innovators, Creatives, Psychology
Junkies, Rebels, Designers, Engineers and people that are very
ambitious.

In addition to this, here are some other reasons you
might have picked this book up.

You like to hear a preceptive on material that comes
from a Jungian Psychology, Personality Type Point of
view.

You have a desire to understand the mechanics behind
movies and human behavior

You could feel like you are being underpaid for your skills are being underutilized and would like to grow in all areas of life.

What we love is inspiration. and the best inspirations come from people's stories.

With the framework of the hero's journey you can learn about in all-encompassing theory of life that follows the human race everywhere we go.

So…

IF you have a desire to create yet you need the encouragement, the empowerment and the inspiration to keep the fire going you will find it here.

For people like us it's a blessing when you feel engaged in the work and a curse when you have to ask others to invest in you.

Investments is always the case with us.

Getting someone to invest in your journey to success, No matter how big or how small from a start-up company to a multi million dollar idea.

We feel stronger with someone in our corner to inspire us, motivate us. Keep us in check and aware that we have the power to do the things we want to do, I reminder of our greatness.

Someone to keep us accountable for our goals and dreams.

We are agents of change, risk takers, adrenaline junkies and live for adventure.

Because of our boundless energy to accomplish all things in relation to our devoted personal or professional goals we have tremendous work ethic.

And will stop at nothing to make it happen. We are resourceful.

So, what we love is inspiration. and the best inspirations come from people's stories.

Everyone has a story. What story are you living?

C H A P T E R 1

The Hero's Journey

**The Hero's Journey is a skeletal framework that
should be fleshed out and filled in
with the details and surprises of you own
individual story**

It is time to… awaken the Hero in your life!
You are the one the world has been waiting
for!

The seed of the hero and all its infinite power has been lying dormant inside you just beneath the surface this whole time! It has been waiting for you to awaken to this truth.

It is within your power to realize that you can be this great hero, with endless resources and wisdom both inside of you and outside of you, but how are you going to do it? You need the right tools and you need to ask the right questions.

Essentially, what is the task of the hero?

"The task of the hero is to claim one's own life and place in the world instead of having one's life and place in the world determined by others"

(*Depth Coaching*, Patrica Adson p. 2).

In others words, live the life of your own choosing!

To give you more clarity, let's refer to the book, *The Human Condition.*

Hannah Arendt in *The Human Condition* cites the distinction that the ancient Greek philosophers made between **'animal' work – the work of a slave** (an animal laborans or laboring animal) necessary to stay alive but leaving no mark behind, sweeping the floor that gets dirty again, cooking the meal that gets eaten –and **'human' work. Human work**, to those Greeks, **the work of free men**, involved courage: the risk of casting one's own being into the arena, in art, political contest, or any game of human skill in which you make your individual mark on your time. The concept of **'hero'** comes from that definition of 'human work.' Originally, it did not necessarily connote great physical bravery but simply the risk of freely chosen tasks or adventure in a community of equals, in which

you dared to expose your true self. [bold added].
(*Depth Coaching*, Patrica Adson p. 5-6)

Here in America we are past the idea of physical slavery but somehow the work of the slave morphed into this idea of mental slavery. We the masses have no chains on our feet, no bindings on our hands but still we can't free ourselves. We may be bound financially, emotionally, spiritually, or mentally.

Because of these bindings it is difficult to take on freely chosen tasks. Accounting makes more more then art. Your parents want you to take a certain direction in life but you don't want to. Yet you don't want to dishonor them by takng the road less traveled, You have a calling or feel energy to do something but can't quite make it happen. Mentally you get distracted often and easily confused. No matter what challenge you have the hero's journey can help you break through the resistance.

The Hero's Journey was first hypothesized by Joseph Campbell in his book *Hero with a Thousand Faces*. It originally had 17 steps and the names of each step were esoteric and complex to say the least. He was definitely the pioneer of the idea and understood how myths, folklore and culture worked like no one else. Then some years later Christopher Vogler tackled this idea of "The Hero's Journey" In his book *The Writers Journey*. He simplified the idea while keeping a majority of its power and complexity intact. He made it into 12 steps and much easier to grasp. The following is from his book.

"The **Hero's Journey** is a skeletal framework that should be fleshed out [and filled in] with the details and surprises of [your own] individual story. The structure should not call attention to itself, nor should it be followed too precisely." (p.19)

In this sense, you are starring in your own movie, playing out the role you choose.

In *The Writer's Journey,* Christopher Vogler provides a simplified and practical guide to the Hero's Journey (p. 19):

1.   Heroes are introduced in **the ordinary world.**

2.   They receive the **call to adventure.**

3.   They are **reluctant** at first or **refuse the call,** but

4.   are encouraged by a **mentor**

5.   **cross the first threshold** and enter the special world.

6.   They encounter **tests, allies, and enemies**.

7.   They **approach the inner most cave,** crossing a second threshold,

8.   where they endure the (central) **ordeal.**

9.   They take possession of their **reward** and

10.   are pursued on **the road back** to the ordinary world.

11.   They cross the third threshold, experience a **resurrection,** and are transformed by the experience.

12.   They **return with the elixir**—a boon or treasure to benefit the ordinary world.

In addition to the twelve steps of the Hero's Journey, there are three main stages:

Departure or Preparation - Preparing for the central ordeal.

Steps 1 through 4 are aligned with preparing for the journey, gathering the necessary resources you need to succeed, and departing from your old ways.

Initiation or Journey – Struggling or pursuing the central ordeal and obtaining the reward.

Steps 5 through 9 are aligned with your private and individual journey, the journey only you fully know. It is also the called a "soul journey," where you find out more about yourself, rely on instincts and push your limits. It is where you turn inward to explore, reflect, fight the dragons, claim your gifts, and discover your strengths and talents.

Return back to the ordinary world – Obtaining the reward of the central ordeal.

Steps 10 through 12 are aligned with returning your gifts to society and playing your functional role in society. The elixir is the reward, insight, gift, **vision**, invention, or new knowledge with which you intend to return and give the people.

To assist you in understanding the Hero's Journey I have made an illustration describing it. Figure 1 will provide a visual for this chapter. This image describes the life-cycle of a dream to fruition; or **Vision in Action**. Notice the ordinary man receives the vision or call to adventure from the great wise man in sky. He then travels into the special world where he finds a mentor. This mentor guides the hero to the completion of his **central ordeal**, which in this case is to stop the dragon from terrorizing the city, behead him, and save the girl.

The Hero's Journey

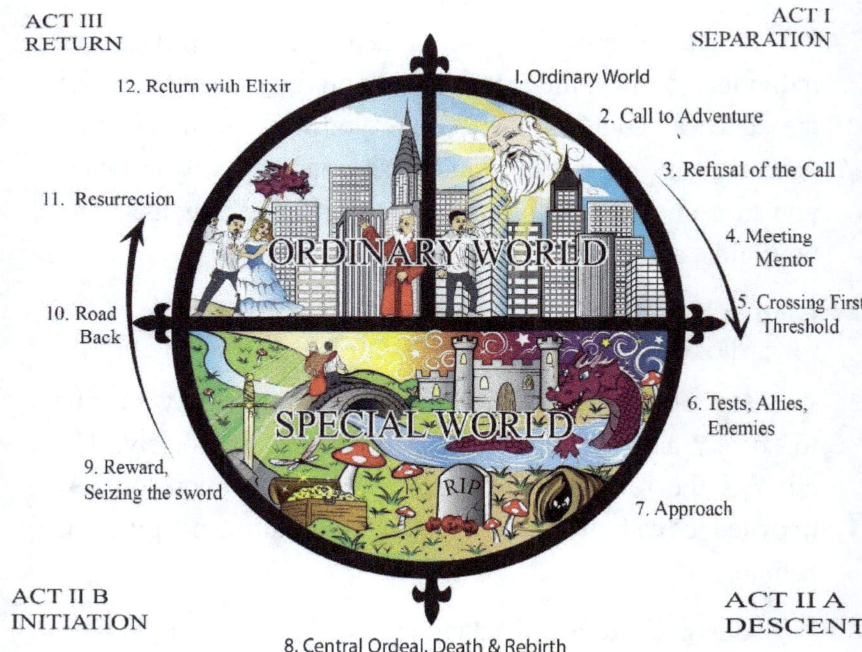

Figure 1

Above is the image describing each stage of the Life-cycle of a person's transformation. Known as the hero's journey. **Remember, you are the hero of your own life; you are the protagonist. The story doesn't move forward unless *you* take action.** To make it easier from here on in, I will be using WJ to refer to the Writer's Journey by Christopher Volger, Third Edition.

My aim is to infuse literary examples with real-world examples so that you can understand this concept from different angles.

Step one- Ordinary world

- The ordinary world is the collective world we all experience, with all of its mundane issues. It houses all our earthly issues. Like in our ordinary world, some things go well, and some do not. To use a literary/film example for something seemingly going well, let us consider the *Lord of the Rings – Fellowship of the Ring*, where Frodo his best friend (Sam) and his two cousins (Merry and Pippin) live merrily and happily in a small village of Shire. To give an example of something going badly, let us look at the case of a failing business, or not having a good career, a girlfriend, a happy marriage, or a good place to live. It sets the stage for the contrast to come. Here are some more examples:

- In Batman comics, the ordinary world is Gotham city, riddled with thieves and gangsters.

- In the Christian Bible, the Israelites are being oppressed, it is a problem they all commonly share, and they all suffer through this and are looking for some way out.

- From a real life point of view, the ordinary world is shown in a variety of TV shows ranging from, *Bar Rescue*, *Restaurant Impossible*, and *The Profit*. What all these shows have in common is that they look to help, save, or make profitable a failing business. In Bar Rescue, people can turn

John Taffer, In Restaurant Impossible, they turn to Robert Irvine, and in the Profit they turn to Marcus Lemonis. The scene is set at the beginning of the show. For example, in *The Profit*, a business owner states, "In the six years owning the restaurant, Standard Burger, we have put in over $250,000 and we have not taken a salary. The restaurant has severely stressed us (the owners) and our family" We hear of their distress and now follows their "call to adventure."

Step two – Call to adventure

- This call to adventure can be like having a vision, having that brief insight into what you want to do with your life or the flash of insight for an invention or an idea to solve your problem. This is particular to each person. Whatever the case, you can no longer stay in the comfort or discomfort of your ordinary world, you need to take action. So, you start on your quest!

- The main purpose here is to fully understand and realize the problem at hand. When you fully understand the problem, solutions emerge.

- "In *Star Wars* the Call to Adventure is Princess Leia's desperate holographic message to wise Obi Wan Kenobi, who asks Luke to join in the quest. Leia has been snatched by evil Darth Vader." (p.10 WJ) Luke Skywalker joins the quest to help save her because he realizes the dire nature of the call.

- Using our previously mentioned TV show *The Profit,* the call is when the failing business-owners of Standard Burger go on a quest to get on the show with Marcus Lemonis.

Step three – Refusal of the call

- Many excuses can frame this refusal to call. "I don't have the funds," "I can't do it," "I don't know anybody," or "I'm not smart enough."

- Here the hero must face uncertainties and doubts. He may be afraid to move on due to previous doubts and this is paralyzing him. The hero needs faith, both in himself and in the process. He cannot let the circumstances control him. He must " walk by faith not by sight"

- In the *Lord of the Rings – Fellowship of the Ring -* Frodo is initially reluctant to leave his comfortable life in Shire, but when he is almost killed by the Ringwraiths (Sauron's minions) he realizes his life will always be at risk as long as the ring exists.

- Returning to our *The Profit* example, the owners of Standard Burger have to send countless emails, calls, and postcards for two years. Imagine the reluctance they might have felt after a year of no response. They might not have wanted to continue, but their persistence eventually did pay off.

Step four – Meeting the Mentor

- **The relationship between hero and mentor is one of the most common themes of all.** It can have many forms; Parent and child, teacher and student, coach and client. The mentor can help in pursuing the change by putting the hero in the right mind-set, asking insightful questions, going in depth with him and using encouragement, but ultimately, it is up to the hero.

- In literature, the mentor is the archetype of the "old wise man" a role that is rich in symbolic value. In most cases, the mentor gives the means to change.

- Making any change is tough; however, it cannot be forced upon the hero. It has to be voluntary. Be wary though if it's a change that needs to happen, you can either be a part of the change or become a victim of it.

- The mentor or coach can also give new light to wrong interpretations and break limiting beliefs.

- It doesn't always have to be one person, for example in the *Lord of the Rings – Fellowship of the Ring*, Frodo meets the Fellowship, who are sworn protectors that have pledged to help Frodo in his quest to destroy the ring. They all play as mentors to Frodo.

- In *The Profit,* the meeting of the mentor (Marcus Lemonis) comes as a response to the owner's persistent communications. Marcus assesses the situation and makes a proposal using his classic criteria "People, Process, and Product." To him this means that you have to have the right people, an efficient process, and an effective product. When the owners accept his proposal and the check he gives them to re-energize their business, then they enter the "special world," where Marcus is 100% in control for the time being.

Step five - Crossing the first threshold into the "special world"

- Here the hero makes the commitment to the adventure. The hero agrees to face the consequences of dealing with the problems or challenges proposed in the call to adventure. He experiments with change and gets comfortable with the new special world eventually becoming acclimated and accepting of the new surroundings. The special world is not the collective ordinary world he or she has left behind, it is very specific to that individual and the challenges he faces.

- "This is the moment when the story takes off and the adventure really gets going" quoted from WJ. You have crossed the first threshold into the special world. There is no turning back from this point.

- "In the *Wizard of Oz* this is moment Dorothy sets out on the yellow brick road," and Frodo begins his quest with the aid of the Fellowship on his long journey to the volcano Mount Doom to destroy the ring.

- This is when John Taffer of *Bar Rescue*, Robert Irvine of *Restaurant Impossible* or Marcus Lemonis of *The Profit* starts to get involved in helping, saving or making profitable the failing business.

Step six --- Encountering Tests, Allies, and Enemies.

- As you progress through the special world you will definitely run into all kinds of tests, allies and enemies. The key to success here is finding people that think the way you do and hold the same values and ideals. Make them your allies. You may also make enemies and meet with "haters," people that don't think your way. You may win some over, and some will stay against you.

- In this "special world," it is likely you will make wrong assumptions and not know where to turn, when this happens you can consult your mentor or coach.

- "In *Stars Wars* [Luke Skywalker goes into] the cantina [or bar] [this] is the setting for the creation of a major alliance with Han Solo and the making of an important enmity [enemy] with Jabba the

Hutt." As quoted from WJ. In the *Lord of the Rings*, Frodo journeys over the mountain pass, merely escapes the wrath of Balrog, he becomes allies with the elves, he is almost captured by the forces of Saruman, he is attacked by Gollum, and he is nearly eaten by a carnivorous Spider.

- In *The Profit* this where Marcus, corrects some of the wrong assumptions, the business-owner has made and he helps them see the situation clearer. In our example, the owners of Standard Burger think they hold the "golden standard" for burgers. When Marcus eats their burger he strongly disagrees. He treats the owners to a burger at another restaurant called *Umami Burger*. They find that the burgers there really are of high quality there.

Step seven --- Approach to the inner most cave

- Here the hero needs to devise a plan to break into the dangerous place which is the inner sanctuary, where the prize resides. The hero must cross the second threshold in order to encounter the central ordeal.

- The strategy needed involves a systematic collection of data from a wide range of sources directed towards the mission requirements. This is needed in order to plan for any or all possible outcomes.

- In some war movies this is where there is a rally of the troops, and action clarification. The people have a clear vision as to what will happen if they win or lose. The generals or leaders send out scouts to gain knowledge about the central ordeal, this is done in order to infiltrate the temple, the specific room of an office building, or secret underground chamber in order to make a plan of attack.

- This step is best described in heist movies, such as *Ocean's Eleven.* Danny Ocean and his 11 accomplices gather information about how to get the $150 million from the safe. They strategize how to break into the safe and grab all the money.

- The seventh step of the hero's journey can also be illustrated in shows like *Bar Rescue* and *The Profit.* In business, "approaching the inner most cave," is like getting detailed information about the demographics of your customers and getting into the mind of your consumers. This is done to provide insight into how you can become more profitable. **This is because the central ordeal of any company is to be profitable**. So, in *Bar Rescue*, they look into the bar location and see the relationship between, the amount of foot traffic, visibility from the street, etc. Similarly you must take action in accordance to the solid data you receive or currently have.

- In the episode about "Standard Burger" from the series *The Profit,* Marcus finds out that restaurant is failing because of the quality of the burger and because of the disharmony of the owners. Marcus has to find a way to approach the problems and find an effective solution for all of them.

Step eight – Central Ordeal!

- "Here the fortunes of the hero hit [rock] bottom, [He is now] in direct confrontation with his greatest fear. He faces the possibility of death and is brought to the brink in a battle with a hostile force. The Ordeal is a "black moment" for the audience, as we are held in suspense and tension, not knowing if he will live or die. The hero, like Jonah is "in the belly of the beast." (Pg.15 WJ)

- This is a critical moment in any story, an ordeal in which the hero must die or appear to die so that he can be born again. It is a major source of the magic of the heroic myth. Emotions run high.

- In film, this is when in *Ocean's Eleven*, we are held in suspense; does the team have the money or not? Did they get away with it? Is everyone okay and alive?

- In real life, this can be seen in the Olympics, the final race to win the gold when the runner is in the final race to win the gold and the audience is waiting for the judges to give them their scores. In competition-style TV shows like *The Biggest Loser*, this is when the contestants do the weigh in.

They don't know how much weight they have lost until it is revealed at the end. It is suspenseful, who will go home and who will stay?

- In the "Standard Burger" episode of *The Profit,* this is when we wonder if Marcus can reconcile the owners and make the business profitable. Can Marcus bring together the fighting owners, and fix all the problems they face?

- In all of these cases above the central ordeal is when the person, business, or contestant confronts their biggest obstacles. It is the suspense that surrounds it that keeps us on the edge of our seat.

Step nine - Reward

- It is a time to celebrate; the hero takes possession of the treasure.

- The reward could be knowledge or great self-realization. The realization that you can do the thing that you thought you couldn't (you realize that you are smart enough, brave enough, etc.) all the reasons in the "refusal of the call to adventure" are now reversed.

- It can be a new found relationship, with business partner, an alliance with a certain group of people.

- In *Ocean's Eleven*, this is when they have finished the job and the bags of money are in their hands.

- In business, this is the opening or reopening of the store of your dreams. In *Bar Rescue,* they sometimes come up with a different name, a completely renovated inside, and it is re-branded.

- In *The Profit*, Marcus harmonizes the owners of Standard Burger and fixes the problem, the store re-opens and it is a now a success.

- It can also be getting your first prototype of your invention up and running then, showing your friends and family at a party with pride.

Step ten - The road back to the ordinary world.

- In psychological terms, this stage represents the resolve of the hero to return to the ordinary world and implement the lessons learned in the special world. This can be far from easy. The Hero is now crossing **the third threshold**. He is now going back to the ordinary world.

- In film, "Some of the best chase scenes spring up at this point, as the hero is pursued…by the vengeful forces she has disturbed by seizing the sword, the elixir, or the treasure" (pg.17 WJ)

- The road back is not an easy one. No one may believe the hero's miraculous escape from death. His or her adventures may be rationalized away by skeptics Despite the skeptics, the hero is determined to try and tell his tale.

- In *The Profit,* This is where Marcus leaves and the owners of Standard Burger have to rededicate themselves to the profitability of their business.

- At this point, a kind of complacency settles in. He is comforted because he has won and he is celebrating however, the hero must replace his inertia with action. Either by his own inner resolve or by an external force.

- This is a point where we are stuck between old ways and new ways and instead of being dependent, we need to realize that we are now interdependence with everything. We know our role and other people's role. Now we need to return back to the community. But the special world is so appealing!

Step eleven – Resurrection

- This is a time of emotional catharsis for the movie – a rededication to the mission.

- You're now resurrected and you have reinvigorated the old sense of self and the old way that you were with a new sense of self and the new things that you learned in your journey. You are transformed into a new being because of your experiences.

- "This is often a second life-and-death moment…Death and darkness get in one last, desperate shot before being finally defeated" (pg.17 WJ)

- In Lord of the Rings, this is the epic battle of Gandalf and the Balrog on the bridge,   where

Gandalf shouts "YOU SHALL NOT PASS!" while Frodo and the others cross the bridge to safety. The Balrog has a desperate shot before falling to its eventual death; he swings his whip and grabs Gandalf's foot. After Gandalf's final words "Fly, you fools!" he falls into the pit with Balrog. He succeeds in getting Frodo one step closer to Mt. Doom to destroy the Ring with this action but appears to die here.

- In business, this is the first week of opening or re-opening the restaurant or business, this is the final "stress test" to see if all the hard work paid off and the problem that was causing the business to fail was fixed. In *The Profit,* Standard Burger has some hiccups with the new structure and business model Marcus has set up for them; they have to make a plan to straight this out.

- In the show, *The Biggest Loser*, the contestants will have to remember all the things they learned during the show, will they internalize it? And will they keep the weight off?

- As you can see there is a possibility of success but there is also a possibility of failure. Have we learned our lessons? Can we apply them? And will they work in the long run?

Step Twelve --- Return with the elixir

- As Vogel reminds us, "The hero returns to the Ordinary world, but the journey is meaningless unless the hero brings back some **Elixir,** treasure, or lesson from the Special World. The elixir is a magic potion with the power to heal…or it simply might be knowledge or experience that could be useful to the community someday. (WJ, p. 18)

- In literature, the elixir, is head of Grendel in the story of Macbeth, symbolizes that the monster is gone and now there is a peaceful city, the city is healed. In Lord of the Rings, it is the return of the ring to the mountain of Mordor, Frodo going back home and peace in the Shire.

- It is whatever token, experience or understanding that you take with you and implement for the rest of your life as a new transformed being.

- In *The Profit,* Standard Burger is back, better than ever with improved meat, better cheese, better buns, a higher quality product overall, plus the family is working much better now, Marcus has harmonized them, finally they are on their way back to profitability they have learned how to make their business a success.

- You have gone through all your steps in your journey and you have accomplished your vision. You are now living in the ordinary world once again. You have brought peace to the land   or success to your business so it's not really ordinary anymore, that is until there is another change that needs to be made and you must face these challenges with the lessons you have learned along the way.

Vogler reminds us here that:

"The Hero's Journey is a skeletal framework that should be fleshed out with the details and surprises of the individual story. The order of the stages given here is only one of the many possible variations. The stages can be deleted, added to and drastically shuffled without losing any of their power.

The values of the Hero's Journey are what's important. The images of the basic version-young heroes seeking magic swords from old wizards, maidens risking death to save loved ones, knights riding off to fight evil dragons in deep caves, and so on—are just symbols of universal life experiences. The symbols can be changed infinitely to suit the story at hand and the needs of the society…

….Modern heroes may not be going into caves and labyrinths to fight mythical beasts, but they do enter a 'Special World' an 'Inmost Cave' by venturing into space, to the bottom of the sea, into the depths of a modern city, or into their own hearts."

(The Writer's Journey, Christopher Vogler, pgs.19-20)

You may be at the point of departure where you are responding to the call to adventure and entering your special world; you may be currently in your special world at the point of tests and trials; or you may be currently facing the ordeal. Or perhaps you are at the stage of the return, trying to bring your gift back to the ordinary world. Whatever stage you're in, this book will guide you through.

Stage One:

Using Mind Maps to Plan Out Goals

The goals most important to you will be in the center of the mind map. Radiating from the center will be all the possible outcomes of your decision.

This is the beginning of the hero's journey; the preparation. At this stage, you are mapping out your vision, making vision boards, creating your business plan, setting goals, and establishing your main motivations towards the central ordeal. In many ways, it is like beginning with the end in mind. You lay out the grand ideas and use backwards planning to plan your steps for future success.

As it relates to The Hero's Journey, you may recall the movie *The Wizard of Oz*. Dorothy, the main character, follows the yellow-brick road to Oz. Similarly, this chapter will assist you in creating your own yellow-brick road to accomplish your vision.

This chapter discusses mind maps, how to create them and their benefits, long-range planning and goal setting. At the end of it you will be able to create your own unique action plan with motivation embedded into it. Finally, you should know yourself well enough and have the courage to make a sustained effort and see it through to the end. The first reference we will look into is Stephen Kraus a Harvard-trained Scientist that separates the science of success from make believe panaceas. He contributes the following thoughts on goals:

Aligning goals within your long-term vision makes goals easier to remember and more on **top of the mind** enabling better time management because you spend more time progressing towards more important outcomes. (*Psychological Foundations of Success*, Stephen J. Kraus, 2003)

Setting up the small steps to success using the SCAMPI goal-setting process

There are a lot of systems people have developed for setting goals. One of the most common is the S.M.A.R.T goal-setting system (Specific, Measureable, Achievable, Realistic, and Time-oriented). Although this system works very well, the one created by Stephen J. Kraus works better. It uses a more advanced goal setting system, because it hits on key points that the SMART system doesn't touch. For example, **Inspiration** and **Approach.** The goal setting system is called S.C.A.M.P.I. Stephen Kraus explains:

SCAMPI = Specific, Challenging, Approach, Measurable, Proximal, Inspirational

This system of goal setting is effective for three main reasons: 1) direction, 2) motivation, and 3) strategy refinement. Each one of the six "SCAMPI" principles makes at least one of those three reasons more prevalent"

S is for Specific. This means ambiguity-reduction, breaking down any vague task, to eliminate wiggle-room. include specific work-based descriptions instead of vague terminology, the more specific the better. Instead of "other leaders" – the leaders names.

C is for Challenging. The goal must be difficult yet attainable. You must find out what you know you can do then seek to stretch yourself further. One only gets stronger when challenged. Just like when you work out in a gym, you need to increase the weight resistance to grow bigger muscles.

A is for Approach. This may be simple, but it is profound. Focus on what you want, not avoiding what you don't want. Here's an example: When speaking about relationships, I hear a lot of people talk about what they don't want. They say, "Well, I don't want a guy that has this quality, or that quality, and oh, he can't like dogs, because I don't like dogs." What you're really doing here is making up avoidance goals—you are avoiding certain characteristics in the person you're looking for. The **approach** and the focus should be on what you want. In driving a golf club, where do you want the ball to go? When driving a car you look at where you want to go, not at the trees passing beside you, unless you want to slam into one of those trees (not advised)!

M is for Measurable. Set up milestones to provide clear, measurable progress. This can be done through a series of little victories that build up like a snowball going downhill, giving you the momentum to achieve more. It's also a great time to celebrate, as a previous win will turn into one more, and another, and another. This enables you to feel as if you have made degrees of success, so that each day is not a pure success or pure failure. Every day is a victory when the measure of the day is shown by its varying degrees. Just one little victory is the spirit of breaking out of that rut and making it a very productive day.

The idea here can be applied to any ambition. Let's say you have a goal of writing a 200-page novel. Some days you write one page and other days you write 10 pages. Each day you write is a victory and the varying degrees are the amount of pages written. You can set the acceptable minimum at five pages a week, 20 pages a month, and over the course of 10 months you will have completed your 200 page novel. It is important to set up measurable, weekly steps so you can see and feel your progress.

P is for Proximal. You have to have a deadline. As the deadline looms, you think more about the goal. Actually, some experience the most productivity time in those last two weeks before the deadline. However, let most things in life you can over do it with planning. If a person's life is controlled only by their work appointments and there is no time set aside to play, reflect or to just do nothing. This can be potentially draining. Research suggests, the best way to plan is weekly, maybe for some, even monthly. The frequency depends on your personality you can be what they call in Myers Briggs personality assessment a "J" and love being scheduled or you can be a "P" where you like your schedule to be more open. The volume of your work deadlines depends on your personality. It's important to know yourself.

I is for Inspirational. The most inspirational goals are those that are self-initiated and consistent with your ideals and ambitions for your future. It has to be important to you and something that **you** actually want to achieve.

If not, then where's the motivation? From the outside? From someone or something outside yourself? If so, then this is extrinsic motivation. Your fulfilling someone else's vision, or dream. This is not so inspiring, unless their dreams and visions are consistent with your own. Finally, not all tasks are fun yet they need to be done, in this case the motivation comes from seeing the big picture. This challenge is a result of being short-sighted. I would suggest finding a way that a seemingly undesirable task will lead up to getting the big picture's central goal. Do something you may not like to do to get that thing you really want.

Now that we finished with SCAMPI and in this last letter we talked about motivation, Let's talk about on what a Vision is and why someone would be motivated to pursue their vision.

What is a Vision?

Conceivably, a vision can be any number of things: a plan for a new structure of an existing company, or brand new company, a visual blueprint of an invention or perhaps a statement of purpose for some job or entity. It can be an individual insight that happens internally and privately or a collective vision for a project. Many times it's a kind of interior mental image that only you can see, unless you express it in a variety of forms. A vision by itself is neutral in nature; it's what we do with it that makes the difference. When we take our focus off our vision and on to the wrong things, it can lead to negative destructive results. Alternatively, if we stay focused on positive growth, value creation education, peace and happiness it will lead to constructive results.

A good example of this in psychology is body image. If we see ourselves as beyond hope, ugly, too fat or too thin and dwell on this it can cause anxiety and depression. On the flip side if we see the challenge, take responsibility for it and think positively, we can change our diet, exercise routine and possibly hang a picture in our room of a certain body image and this would motivate us. Having a solid vision of what we want will keep us moving forward!

Why would you want to pursue your vision?

A vision is an intrinsic goal by its very nature; it is something that comes from you internally. Pursuing and achieving this vision will provide you with **happiness** and of course it would mean you are making your own individual mark in this lifetime as well.

Pursuing a dream or vision is something to which only you can assign and interpret value to. It offers immeasurable worth, not material worth. Unlike money, the value is not printed on it.

Extrinsic vs intrinsic goals and happiness:

In the film, "Happy," Psychology Professor Tim Kasser brings up the two basic types of goals we have as human beings: **intrinsic** and **extrinsic**. He notes that people with intrinsic goals are concerned with "personal growth, creating and sustaining relationships and desire to help the community. [They] report being happier, having more vitality, and feeling less depression and anxiety…Intrinsic goals are inherently satisfying in and of themselves, they have to do with intrinsic psychological needs that we all, as people, have." (*Happy,* film, 2011)

He contrasts this with extrinsic goals such as, "money, image, and status goals, which we all want to some degree. But people that are more oriented to money, image, and status tend to report "less satisfaction with their lives, they were more depressed and anxious, they felt less vitality and less energized in their day-to-day life." (*Happy,* film, 2011)

From the above insights you can see that intrinsic goals will make you happier than extrinsic goals. The vision comes from inside you, and now you want to bring that vision into action. The challenge here is to have time to create it and follow through with it. Therefore it is important to have work/life balance. When a life is based on constant work, you do not have time for happiness. Constant work can be defined as something you like doing and can't stop doing,   working solely for money to pay off debts, or working for image and status (extrinsic goals). For many people in these cases, it is simply working too many hours; others overwork in order to live up to image or social status requirements.

It could be, then, that we as a people are so wrapped up in meeting these extrinsic goals that we do not make the time to achieve our intrinsic goals. Or, we simply disregard our intrinsic goals. These can be enriching one's personal growth, having hobbies, building relationships, and desiring to help the community. Instead, we tend to achieve extrinsic goals such as earning money or gaining image, social status, or popularity. Whatever the reason, the fallacy in this mentality is that if you do not have the intrinsic activities in place, chances are you do not have work/life balance, and thus you are not happy.

More on Intrinsic goals:

Let's take drumming as an example of an intrinsic goal. Playing in a group can build relationship with others. Playing new rhythms, being able to play faster, being adaptable enough to change rhythms quickly, and being able to keep the beat or leave space for other musicians are all signs of personal growth in drumming. If you're doing this hobby with others you have known for a while, it increases the happiness exponentially with each person involved. The key to this is balance. If you focus all your time and energy on making money all day, every day, you leave no time for personal growth outside of work. There is no time to play with others, (drumming, writing, exercise, etc.), and no time to build relationships at home with family, friends, or significant others. You're what they call a "workaholic." It is doubtful that you are happy.

Conversely, if you're a travelling musician or a new artist playing gigs everywhere you can, and you're not getting paid enough to play, you could be happy just introducing your talent to the masses, but you are struggling to make ends meet, this puts a damper on your happiness.

The age-old question - does money buy happiness?

In regards to money, research suggests that past a certain point, money cannot buy you happiness anymore. This research has been reviewed and written about in articles ranging from Time, Forbes, and all the other major news channels. This magical point is $75,000.

The research I am talking about is one published by Dr. Kahneman, 2002 Nobel prize-winning psychologist and Dr. Deaton 2015 Nobel prize-winning economist both from Princeton University.

"They analyzed responses to the Gallup-Healthways Well-Being Index (GHWBI), a daily survey that asks roughly 1,000 U.S. residents a battery of questions about their wellbeing. After analyzing more than 450,000 GHWBI responses from 2008 and 2009, Dr. Deaton and Dr. Kahneman found that happiness is actually the result of the fulfillment of two abstract psychological states -- emotional well-being and life evaluation"

"Of all the important and interesting findings Dr. Kahneman and Dr. Deaton's research has uncovered, the most reported finding is that people with an annual household income of $75,000 are about as happy as anyone gets."

"No matter where you live, your emotional wellbeing is as good as it's going to get at $75,000," says Dr. Deaton, "and money's not going to make it any better beyond that point. It's like you hit some sort of ceiling, and you can't get emotional well-being much higher just by having more money."

(Robison, Jennifer. "Happiness Is Love -- and $75,000, Gallup.com)

So what is happiness and how do we find it?

Ultimately, the path to true happiness lies within oneself, interacting with others and building relationships with others, towards positive growth.

To give some final thoughts on happiness, I would like to cite a concept titled "Relative Happiness and Absolute Happiness" from SGI's *An Introduction to Buddhism:*

The SGI, which stands for Soka Gakkai Internatioal, is a Buddhist organization that promotes value creation education, peace, culture and happiness

Second Soka Gakkai president Josei Toda taught that there are two kinds of happiness: relative happiness and absolute happiness. Relative happiness speaks of a condition in which one's material desires or immediate personal wishes are satisfied. While there is no limit to what we can hope or wish for, there is always a limit to what we can have materially and how long we can hold onto it. For example, we may get something we want at this moment, but the fulfillment we enjoy from getting it will not last... should those circumstances change or disappear, so will our happiness. Such happiness is called relative because it exists only in relation to external factors. [If such factors are gone, so goes our happiness]

In contrast, absolute happiness means that living itself is happiness; being alive is a joy, no matter where we are or what our circumstances. It describes a life condition in which happiness wells forth from within. It is called absolute because it is not influenced by external conditions. **Attaining Buddhahood means developing absolute happiness.** [bold added] (pg.28 -29)

Todei, continues to comment on the concept of "happiness":

Beyond the troubles of just getting by in life, we often face unexpected problems. Happiness does not depend on whether or not we have problems, but how we perceive and deal with them. To cite an analogy, a person of little strength and experience who encounters a steep mountain path will view it as a daunting obstacle. But a strong, experienced hiker can confidently ascend a steep trail even while carrying a heavy backpack, enjoying the view along the way. In a similar way, one who has firmly established a life condition of absolute happiness can confidently face any difficulty. Problems can even become an impetus to bring forth a powerful life force, enabling one to calmly and confidently overcome any challenge.

Josei Toda final comments are:

"For a strong mountain climber, the steeper and more rugged the mountain, the greater the enjoyment. Likewise, a person who has developed the wisdom and life force to

overcome hardship will find society, which is rife with problems, to be a place for the creation of value and fulfillment." (pg.29)

Following this guidance should give you an understanding of happiness, peace, and balance. It will also give you encouragement to go on the hero's journey and accomplish whatever vision you have.

Lastly, be wary of making goals when in a negative mood as Stephen Kraus explains:

When in negative moods, people set unrealistically high goals because they are focused on how well they would have to perform to make themselves feel better. Needing to achieve a lot to feel happy, they set overly ambitious goals." (*Psychological Foundations of Success,* Stephen Kraus, p. 95)

Goals should be made in a positive frame of mind. Anything less than that will lead to mediocre levels of success and unattainable goals. A **positive mood is a requirement.**

The SCAMPI systems, together with the creation of a mind-map, form the basis of the strategic plan of action that can be used to help you achieve your goals and dreams!

What I learned about goal setting after I applied it to coaching

Goals are made to keep us on track with our planned direction. It's a form of planned change and organized development.

To keep the goal's progress there needs to be the intrinsic motivation striving towards that goal.

The mechanics of this are: First, the **dis-satisfaction or the internal desire to grow/elevate/create** the current conditions in your life, family, business or relationship. As such, the motivation for the change comes from within. The next step after that is **search and analyze.** Looking for the correct solutions to your specific desire or problems. **Goal setting** this way has motivation embedded into it. All that is left is the follow through. We have now come to **implementation and strategy refinement.** The actual implementation is a lot easier, if there is goal consensus and everyone is unified around the same central goal. As the goals are completed, challenges may come up and may be a cause for strategy refinement. This is done on a one to one basis.

Create your mind map with your central goal and supporting small steps

A mind map can also be used as a long-range view of what needs to get done. The best part is that you can always add to your mind-map as more connections or associations toward your goal come up. It could also be used as a brainstorming tool. Let's say you're looking to grow your business. You can write down all the possible ways you can promote your business, various possible directions will emerge. The more you write down, the greater the possibility of getting something that really works for you and your business.

Let's refer back to *Bar Rescue* and *The Profit* TV shows we referenced in chapter 1. If these businesses wanted to put down on paper their ideas for marketing, it might look like this… (see figure 2 below)

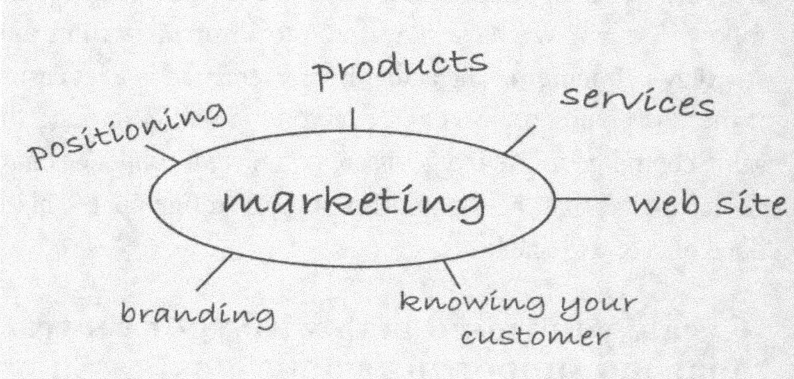

Figure 2

Mind maps integrate all your major action ideas and thoughts into one picture.

When creating a mind map it is wise to first create a strategic frame of mind. The first step in creating this strategic frame of mind is inferred in this quote from Henry David Thoreau:

If one advances confidently in the direction of his dreams, and endeavors to live that life

which he has imagined, he will meet with success unexpected in common hours. If you have built castles in the air, your work need not be lost, that is where they should be. Now put the foundations under them. (*Walden,* Henry David Thoreau)

In this quote from Thoreau, there is a contrast between what you imagine (castles in the air) and what your present reality is. (The foundations under them)

In other words, in order to create this strategic frame of mind, you must contrast the future and the present reality. Looking at one or the other alone isn't really helpful. Doing this leads to mediocre levels of commitment and motivation across the board, for realistic and unrealistic goals alike. But the fusion of the two future and present is powerful. When you look at this contrast, it leads to an outstanding level of commitment and motivation. You set more goals, make more plans, get more deeply committed more quickly, persist longer, and perform better. This is quite a list, but it happens once you do this exercise the correct way. Fantasize first, then focus on reality. This process will fuel the optimistic, yet realistic mindset that is necessary for strategic thinking.

Although this essentially encourages "day-dreaming" this is what Albert Einstein used to call "thought experiments." Doing this helps create your big picture or central idea when making your mind map. After you have defined it, write down all the ideas for action you have about this central idea. The more possibilities you can develop, the greater probability you will find one that resonates with you.

Joseph Campbell expressed this process like a tree growing.

> The tree doesn't know where it's growing next. A branch may grow out this way, then that way, and then another way. If you just let it be and don't have pressures from outside, when you look back, you'll see that this has all been an organic development. (*Reflections on the Art of Living,* Joseph Campbell, p. 70)

As Campbell suggests, write down all the different ways you can accomplish your central goal. Creating this tree of possibilities will bring forth the one right path for you to achieve success.

Keep in mind with the idea of organic development, no choice is a wrong choice as long as it's your choice and you have thought it out carefully.

A connection between the mind map and Jung's Mandala's

A mind map has multiple uses. It's a brainstorming tool to help you take action. It can be used for self-analysis, and can even be used for decision making. It uses pictures, numbers, and shapes in a process called "patterning" to visualize the things you want in your life.

Obviously, Carl Jung was into self-analysis; After all, he is the father of Analytical Psychology. You will see him in figure 3 pointing to the center of a mandala. Jung used mandalas as a sort of therapy, a sort of art therapy if you will. Mandalas have a reconciling ability in of itself. When looking at a mandala professionally done, you see a pattern and a natural order emerge.

Here is a definition from Blake W. Burleson:

> **A Mandala is a symbol of oneness, totality, or integration**. Typically, it is used for meditative visualization among various religious traditions while expressing unity, the alternating quadrants within are meant to depict the dualistic but complementary principles of the universe (*Pathways to Integrity*, Blake W. Burleson, p. 60).

Many people and cultures have vouched for the mandala's intrinsic meaning. Buddhists, Tibetans, and Hindus have all derived meaning from the mandala and its captivating beauty. Jung went as far as calling it "a representation of the unconscious self." The mandala is widely recognized as a meaningful reflection of its creator.

In Jungian psychology, this unconscious self holds your full potential. It is the center source, everything comes to life from this idea of "self." What mandalas have in common with mind maps is that they both have a center from which everything flows. The center of the mind map is like the human heart pumping the life blood into the rest of the body. As you can see, there is also a sense of layering outward. The center illuminates the entire image; one must look at the center first, and then you can understand the rest of the image. In this way, everything coming from the center is just a manifestation or aspect of the center.

In short, I suggest that mind maps be modeled after the design of a mandala. Here in Figure 3, I have a picture of Jung pointing to the center of a mandala reinforcing the importance of the center.

Figure 3

Tibetan Mandalas are unique in the sense that they tell us something using ancient images, colors, symbols, shapes, that words cannot convey. Figure 4 below is a color example of a Tibetan Buddhist Mandala that is similar to the one Jung could have been pointing to. Notice the deity in the center and the smaller deity images around it.

Figure 4

Now, let's look at a couple of examples of mind maps. First, we have Figure 5 inspired by *The Mind Map Book* by Tony Buzan and Barry Buzan (2009). This mind map is meticulously detailed. We will not be doing all the weighting out on our maps but notice the design.

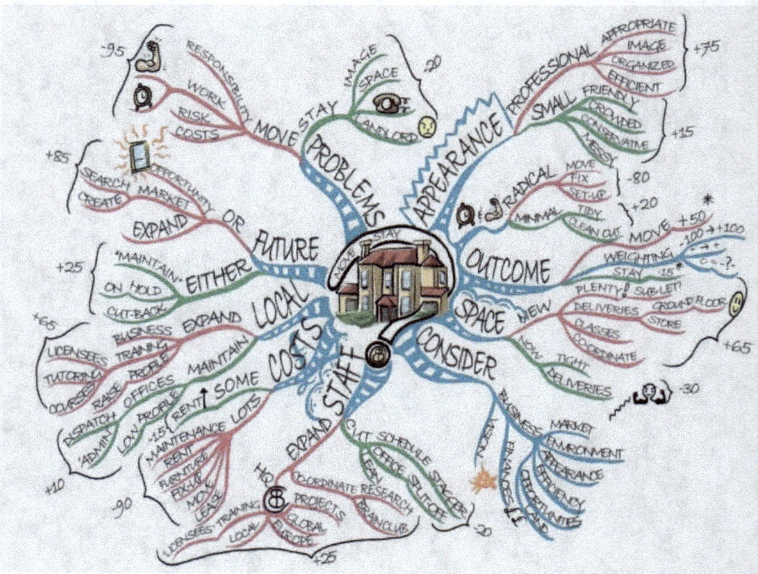

Figure 5

The "Big Central ordeal" here is to "Move or Stay,"

This is what I call a decision map. The decision map drawn out here is analyzing if a female business owner should *stay* at her home based business or *move* to a office, a separate real-estate location. After she carefully weighted her options using the above mind map. It became apparent to her that the correct decision was to move.

What Is Decision Mapping?

Decision Mapping allows you to paint a picture of your pivot-or-preserve moment in a scientific and structured way. It gives entrepreneurs and people in career transition alike the power to choose wisely. It's like putting all your lego pieces on the table and deciding how to build your empire.

This process is aimed towards channeling your vision, intuition and judgement so you can take better action.

Let's break it down specifically looking at the details of

As, discussed this is a female business owner that was trying to decide whether she should move into an office building or continue as a home-based business. In the shape of a Venn type diagram or mind map, the title of the dilemma was in the center. Then, spokes radiating from the center detailed all the worries or determining factors to consider. Such factors were as follows:

- How would her business grow in the **future** if she moved?
- How **Local** would the building be from her current house?
- Who would be the **staff** in the new office?
- How much would it **cost** to rent the office space?
- How much **time and energy** would be involved in making the transition from home-based to office space?
- What would the **appearance** be to other clients?

The decision map had the words in bold in a circle around the central ordeal. When writing it out her answers came out of the words in bold. To indicate her value judgement on those sections in bold she would give a number from 1 to 10. This could be a positive number or a negative number for each factor and, at the end, you would add up all the numbers to give you a final result.

This aided in her decision to move or stay. After all was considered, the final result was that she was going to move. Decision maps can be simple or more involved depending on the situation.

Organize Your Ideas and Prepare for Action

The purpose of this exercise is to provide organization and integration of the main ideas toward action. This should be a fun exercise. You can design your life using it, a life of your conscious choosing.

As opposed to a single graphic organizer with a central theme and spokes all related to the central theme, mind maps go in a lot deeper. You can use images, and draw lines connecting ideas to the different factors. Overall, it is more personally oriented.

Decision mapping is just one tool used in deciding what direction to take in your career path. There are many other tools that can be used to aid you in finding that happy place. Will you take the first step and make it happen? It all depends on you.

This decision mapping is a holistic way of evaluating a decision, much better than a pros and cons list. The mind map actually explains the pains and gains.

Lastly, notice the similarity in design, where the mandala (figure 4) has the deity at the center. The mind map (figure 5) has an image of home-based business and the words "move or stay" between it.

Then, in figure 4 the central deity gets split up into eight smaller deity's, circling around it. Similarly, in figure 5 the mind- map gets broken-down into nine key criteria. The key criteria are specific to this individual's decision making process towards moving or staying with the home-based business. They are underlined in blue in the mind-map and also in chart under the mind map. They are rated by their importance on a scale of   -100 to +100. These numbers can be seen after the brackets. Before the brackets you can see the work he did to get to those numbers.

ITEM	M	S
PROBLEMS	-95	-20
FUTURE	85	25
LOCAL	65	10
COST	-90	-15
STAFF	25	-20
SPACE	65	-30
TIME/ENERGY	-80	20
APPEARANCE	75	15
TOTALS	50	-15

Figure 6

In Figure 6, the M in column 1 stands for Moving (moving the business) and S in column 2 stands for Staying (keeping the business where it is). As you can see, when you look at the totals, it becomes apparent the correct decision is to move.

Mind maps do not have to be complicated or meticulously detailed as the one above. The purpose is to provide organization and integration of the main ideas toward

Lets Look at the center of another mind map this is a self-analysis mind map   (figure 7) and see how everything is connected and associated with it, flowing out in three layers. As you look back at the mind map "to move or stay home" (Figure 5) you will also notice that everything connected and associated with it is flowing out in multiple layers.

Note that Figure 7 shows an example of a "Self-Analysis Mind Map." This example is more geared toward understanding the different aspects of your life. The center is a pictorial illustration of you.

Self-Analysis Mind Map

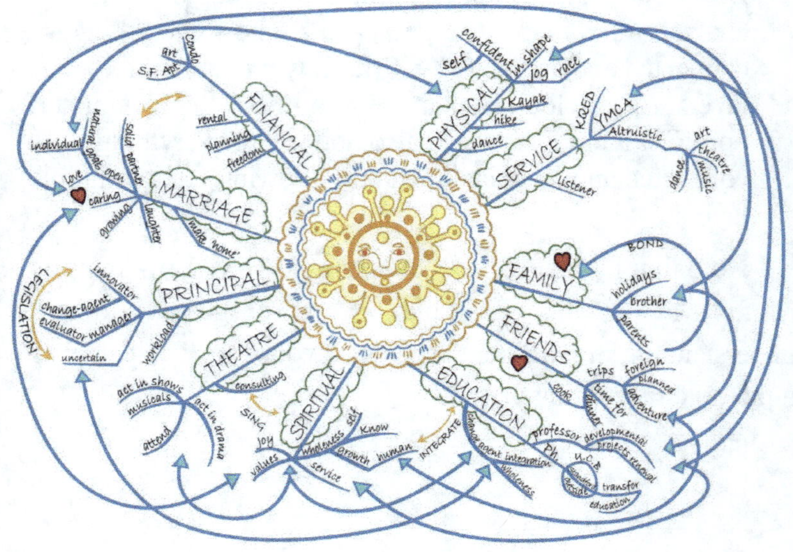

Figure 7

This mind map was also inspired by *The Mind Map Book* by Tony Buzan and Barry Buzan (2009).

From the biggest abstract picture of your life to the concrete details, this self-analysis mind map is quite grand; you can effectively map out your whole life on one sheet of paper.

This kind of mind map can be personalized for you. The words in the ten green clouds in figure 7 are ten directions in which your life can be going in. Sort of like a wheel of life, You can write out ten categories that are intentionally general and abstract so you can break it down and input the details.

Of course, it is a lot easier being guided through it then reading it about it. During a private coaching session I can guide you through a wheel of life assessment.

The criteria for assessing this wheel of life

1. Your rating of satisfaction with this direction.

2. At least three descriptions of how things are now.

3. At least three descriptions regarding how you would like to see things in the future.

The last two items represent a factual readout and a vision for the future, contrasting the ideal with the actual.

The quote that comes to mind is if you build castles in the sky, your work need not be lost for now you must put foundations under them.

This helps you review the past and project future goals.

Like Figure 7 illustrates, you can also mark interconnections between fields with arrows connecting them.

Small pictures such as the three mini red hearts can denote subjects that are dear to your heart. Drawing a little bear under a life direction can mean you want to "bear" with it, a request for forbearance or patience. You can even draw a small bomb under a certain section representing a positive or negative situation. By positive, you are indicating the section is about to blow up; you will gain awareness, popularity, success, growth. By negative, you are indicating the section needs immediate attention because it's about to fall apart or you are getting aggravated, and you might one day **blow up** with anger.

You may be asking yourself who created this self-analysis mind map in figure 7 and what was the benefit of using it?

Let's read on to find the answer the authors of the *Mind Map* book explain:

A chief executive in a multinational corporation who originally wished to analyze his life in relation to his business activities. However, as a mind map increasingly revealed his feelings, and began to reflect all the major elements in his life, they included family, business, sporting activities, learning and general self-development, and his interest in Eastern philosophies and practices.

He subsequently explained that, before the mind mapping self-analysis, he had assumed his business to be his prime concern. But, through mind mapping, he realized that his family was a true foundation of his life, and as a result he transformed his relationship with his wife, children and other relatives. Realizing that, he adjusted his schedule to reflect his true priorities.

Predictably enough, his health and his mental state improved enormously, his family became much closer and more loving, and his business improved dramatically as it began to reflect his new positive outlook. *(The Mind Map Book,* Tony Buzan and Barry Buzan, p. 181.)

Benefits of self-analysis mind maps

1. "They provide a comparatively and interestingly objective perspective on the self.

2. They provide both macroscopic and microscopic views of the individual, encompassing broad trends as well as small but nevertheless relevant details.

3. They make future planning easier and more accurate by putting it in the context of the individual's present state.

4. They act as a permanent record, thus allowing the mind mapper to gain a truer perspective over the long-term.

5. By using colors, images and codes, and to make it easy to express emotions and incorporate them in self-analysis."

>   *(The Mind Map Book,* Tony Buzan and Barry Buzan, p. 182.)

Benefits of Mind Mapping in general

Use mind maps:

✓ If you ever find yourself becoming overwhelmed trying to remember and manage large amounts of information, the mind map holds it all together on one page (similar to a flow chart.)

✓ If you have trouble organizing, mind maps can help you with that. Mind maps hold all the important pieces of information you are looking for in one big picture.

✓ If you struggle to remember key concepts and critical pieces to your academic, business, or career success, the mind map connects them into one comprehensive image.

✓ If you want to align with your brain's natural working pattern and maximize the way you learn, think, and create. Mind maps connect ideas of action to your big agenda items.

✓ If you are creating your own big picture or long-range plan, and you are establishing your central ideas, then creating the small steps to success.

✓ If the breakdown of exactly how to get the destination motivates you and you would like to graphically express the pros and cons or pains and gains of a situation.

Now that you have read both Chapter one and Chapter two.

It's time to take out a journal and write out what you liked most .

53

In chapter one, what stage of the hero's journey are you in?
If you can't pick a stage, pick an act . Act I , II, III.

In Chapter two, which one of the mind maps where most applicable for you ?
The decision mapping one or the self analysis mind map.

I use the SCAMPI process to write resume how else can it be applied?

The Importance of Listening

**_This is the kind of listening you use
when you care deeply about someone,
using compassion and empathy._**

For the success of the hero's vision and mission, it is vital that he not only understands the art of listening but also masters it. He has to listen to hear the call to adventure. There are many forms of listening, Listening to your heart, listening to your inner wisdom, listening for intention these are all touched on throughout the book and important to the hero's journey.

For the purposes of this chapter, listening comes in three important forms: _Intuitive Listening, Egoless Listening and the combination of the two._ When you combine the two forms of listening, it produces the most amazing results. The whole is greater than the sum of its parts.

The technique is to listen to promote, grow, and strengthen, without judgment. Allow for a free-flow of ideas, judgment will stop another person's mind wheels from turning. Great listening is a powerful and freeing experience.

Intuitive Listening

Intuitive listening includes listening for the meaning behind words, understanding tonality, and speech patterns (speaking fast, slow, space between pauses). Making connections in this way is part of this powerful form of listening. The other part is taking that raw information and applying it in a way to promote and grow the individual. It's the kind of listening you use when you care deeply about someone and want to really know what they are saying. You ask *clarifying questions* to understand the meaning behind the other person's words. You polish ideas until they are shiny and bright. Eventually they are just like diamonds.

When using intuitive listening, it is typically good to follow-up with your interpretation of what the person is saying, to clarify whether your understanding is on point or not. Jumping around is fine provided there is a common ground for communication. Be sure to adapt your communication style to the different personality types to ensure clarity. There will be further discussion on personality types in chapter 4 - 6

Egoless Listening

The other important skill in mastering the art of listening is egoless listening. Steven Covey in his book, *Seven Habits of Highly Successful People*, has a great lesson on "egoless listening." He advises, "First seek to understand, then *to be understood.*" Instead of trying to understand what someone else says from your own perspective, put away any of your own pre-conceived ideas, projections, or thoughts. Just listen to them as if you are them, as if you are one. This makes it "egoless," and it is done so you can step into the other person's shoes.

Egoless listening is in stark contrast with ego-centric listening, which describes individuals concerned with "what's in it for me?" and "what am I getting out of this?" This puts up a divider between you and the other person and makes the other feel disingenuous, disconnected, and not unified. It's as if you really don't care what they have to say. You're just waiting for how you are involved, and what you will have to do. In ego-centric listening, what matters is that you get what you want, whatever preconceived notion you have thought before actually speaking….regardless of the consequences.

When using ego-less listening, in contrast, you may even put someone else's concerns before your own. You seek to move as a unit and live harmoniously. You want to cooperate and co-create. You take the time to share their ideas and encourage buy-in with others. That person becomes adaptable and welcomes change as you listen to them.

To sum it up, the best listeners embody the Buddhist saying *"Form is emptiness and emptiness is form."* When listening to the person they become like water poured into a sophisticated container. Assuming the other's personality temporally to see things from their viewpoint. They are able to walk in each person's shoes, as if each person were a different complex-shaped glass, taking the form of the glass and returning back to themselves.

As a literary example, I have chosen the film, *Citizen Kane* to contrast ego-less listening with this classic example of ego-centric listening:

In the film *Citizen Kane*, Charles Foster Kane has earned a fortune from his newspaper business. He goes out into the streets to find a woman of the world and enters a bar where he sees Susan Alexander singing and dancing, trying to make a living in the business of art.

He's intrigued and wants to help her. He perceives her mission in life is to perform on the stage. She needs lessons, he enjoys her artistry, and that's what he wants her to be able to do.

So, without much communication about what she wants to do, he starts to fund this perceived mission. He arranges for dancing lessons, gets her voice lessons, and puts money into developing her skills.

As the movie progresses, he buys her lavish gifts. Eventually, she is fed up and is about to leave him. Charles tells her, "You can't do this to me!"

Susan replies, "Everything is about you! The dancing lessons, you wanted me to do, the voice lessons you wanted me to do."

You see, Charles Kane never directly asked her what she wanted before he invested in the lessons. Their wants and needs where not aligned. They were not working as a couple, because, among other things, they were not completely hearing each other out. Charles only heard what he wanted to hear not what Susan really was saying.

Charles Kane is a great example of the ego-centric concept, and how it is applied to listening. Seek to use ego-less listening instead of ego-centric listening because it leads to harmony and alignment with your

partner.

The Benefits of Intuitive and Egoless Listening with a Transformational Coach

Intuitive and egoless listening allows you to be more *confident, clear,* and *secure* in the direction you are going in life. With this technique, a Transformational Coach can solve two problems, one, **Ambiguity** and two **Ambivalence.** First, they listens freely and without judgment, fleshing out any vague ideas for action by making them more specific or marking them down for not being clear. Then, they empowers you to decide based on a clear vision of the future, you both understand and share. The result is that it makes what was once vague into something specific and detailed. It makes what was once something you were insecure about, secure and more confident. These are the key skills the Transformational coach employs.

Using these skills and techniques of listening there are many health benefits that include:

- ✓ Less stress and doubt

- ✓ Reduced anxiety and worry

- ✓ Continual forward motion and less stagnation

✓ Removal of ruminations (the feeling of paralysis by analysis)

✓ Removal of negative emotions

✓ Alleviated indecisiveness

Out of all these items on this list, "removal of ruminations" will be the one you get most benefit from. Followed closely b y its partner in crime, ambivalence (indecisiveness). Rumination means essentially going to war with yourself; it is when you are in conflict with your own dream. Rumination is one of the most important to address, because it's what holds us back significantly. Stephan Kraus declares that to be an achiever you must take action:

"This pattern of rumination spending more time *thinking* about your goals and less time *taking action* towards your goals. is a characteristic of underachievers, and a number of other groups that you would rather not belong to" (*Psychological Foundations of Success*, Stephen J. Kraus, p. 44)

What is ambivalence and how to find clarity

Ambivalence is the impulse to keep things undecided on and up in the air. To give you a clear understanding of ambivalence and more objectivity on these barriers to success, let's look at Shakespeare's *Hamlet*. Even after hundreds of years, it is still an exceedingly accurate character study of the psychological effects of ambivalence and rumination. You, like Hamlet, might have similar struggles.

"Hamlet is the Prince of Denmark, son of the King. Hamlet's uncle murders the King –his own brother – and marries the Queen. Killing one's brother and marrying his wife is a crime of biblical proportions, and Hamlet swears revenge, vowing to kill his murderous and (by some definition incestuous) uncle. But, Hamlet was plagued by ambivalence; he wasn't certain what he really wanted, or if he could truly bring himself to kill his uncle. And with Hamlet's ambivalence comes a pattern we would expect based on psychological research: anxiety, angst, rebellion, restlessness, procrastination, rumination, and inability to act. (They didn't call him 'the melancholy Dane' for nothing). Throughout the play, he encounters opportunities to take revenge upon his uncle, but he passes each one up, showing the classic ruminative combination of talking endlessly about his goals, but not taking action to accomplish them. Ambivalence and the lack of a clear vision even drive Hamlet's most famous characteristic: the tendency to engage in long, ponderous monologues about vaguely relevant topics. Now, modern readers may read this famous Shakespearean play and marvel at its beautiful choice of words, but at the same time, impatiently implore 'Hamlet, buddy, do something. Anything! Just take action!!!' …. Ambivalence leads to rumination, and rumination leads to a downfall. Hamlet's inaction causes him to lose control of his future and fall victim to the schemes of others. Shakespeare's message: If you don't know where you're going, you leave your destiny to chance."

(Psychological Foundations of Success, Stephen J. Krauss, p. 45)

Don't leave your destiny to chance: **Take action!**

When considering your direction in life, you want someone who will break down your ambivalence and help you find clarity; someone who will sit down with you and evaluated deeply the different directions you might want to go; and flesh out different ideas you have without imposing their will on you, leading you in the wrong direction, motivated by their own personal agendas. You want someone who is actually going to listen to you with the intent of understanding, not just replying, especially to those far-fetched ideas or career directions that are condemned for their impracticality!

When looking for such a guide along the way use the scroll on the next page as a scoring board. See how well your intended partner measures up to it. Your guide should have these skills and know how to use them.

The scroll on the next page organizes five techniques used in intuitive and egoless listening. The scroll has the Chinese symbol that represents listening at the top. Within the symbol there are five parts. Each part is described in the scroll.

It works somewhat like an acronym, but it doesn't use individual letters that represent words. Instead, it uses individual symbols that represent ideas. Notice that each of

the five parts are necessary for complete egoless and intuitive listening;

- The Ear,
- The Heart,
- The Ten Eyes,
- The One, Undivided Attention
- The King

These are all parts of the whole.

If you look closely at figure 7, what the listening symbol is really doing is holding all the important different pieces of information together, like a completed picture puzzle. When you separate the picture into its different symbols, they each have a distinct meaning. Together, they have one meaning. The whole is greater than the sum of its parts.

Summary of Intuitive and Egoless Listening

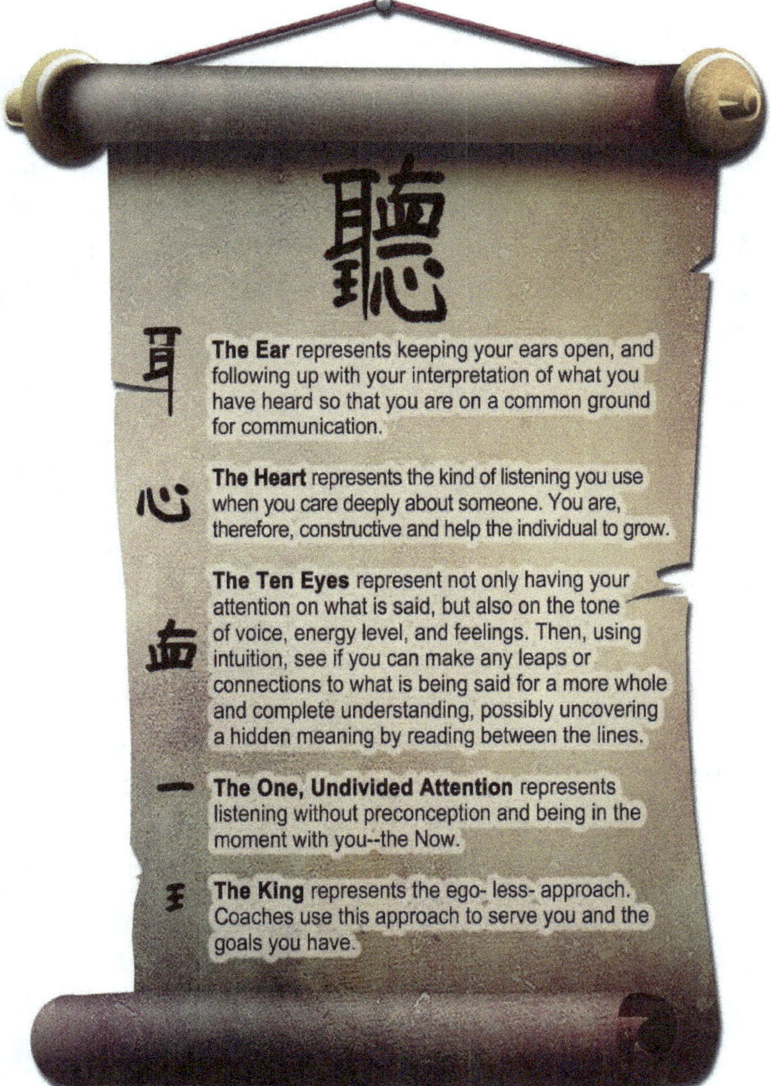

Figure 7

Gain the clarity to take action!

Imagine a building with ten floors and ten rooms on each floor. The name of this building is "Psychology," but you can fill it in with your chosen field of study. Each room represents a different job title within the building's name. The question is this: Which room do you choose? Using a support team that has skills in intuitive and egoless listening is the difference between being on the bottom floor (perhaps wondering who stole your red stapler!) or finding yourself in the upper corner penthouse suite.

Figure 8

Using the right support system is important. Choosing the right people to work with can make a difference. Often guidance and career counselors don't have the intuitive and egoless listening component. Sometimes they may even condemn a dream because of its impracticality.

Many do not listen, and they will make unnecessary prejudgments. They may even say things such as, "there's no money in that" or "there's no use for art here ." This is not constructive; it is destructive and breaks people down. Support should help build people up. If a dream does not seem possible, at the very least offer some suggestions or alternatives that will inspire.

We are boundless and can do just about anything if there is enough emotional engagement and passion. As a Career Coach myself, I often ask, "If money were no object, what career would you choose?" I use the response as a starting point.

A good example is the life story of Joe Ades, a man in a thousand dollar suit who sold his $5 potato peelers on New York City street corners six days a week, ten hours a day. Joe Ades lived in a luxurious Park Avenue apartment and paid for his kids to go to college. The only business in which he ever engaged in was selling his peelers on the streets of Manhattan. People told him it was impossible, but when they said this, he just didn't listen. In Joseph Campbell's words, "He followed his bliss." Joe Ades realized what Campbell realized, "What others think of me must be put aside for bliss."

From the story of Joe Ades, you can see it's important to do whatever you are engaged to do. Just do it sincerely, with all your heart, and be engaged in the activity.

To further enhance your progress to your goals, working with a support system is most beneficial. In the next chapter, we will discuss the support systems available to you.

C H A P T E R 4

Creating Partnerships

***We all need help from others.
Frankly, it is difficult to imagine
any success story
without the help of somebody else.***

In the hero's journey, our hero is now close to approaching the first threshold going into the special world. We have talked about some key elements in the previous chapter however, there are still more aspects of an ideal support system to give guidance. The chapter will go into detail about the four qualities to look for in a transformational coach. Primarily this is on balancing out your decision-making process with a good mentor and how the synergy of two people should look like. I will bring up several movie references and stories of people to do this.

Towards the end of the chapter, I talk about the real crux of the matter as it relates to this step of the hero's Journey. Asking for what you need. Recognizing that you are a particular individual and there is only one of you, what you need can be different than what someone needs.

What does an ideal support system look like?

In the search for an ideal support system, it will be beneficial for you (the hero) to have someone who can crystalize decision-making, someone who can enable you to make the transition from one attitude or life condition to another, and someone who is a good listener. That person should be able to help you overcome your many challenges, trials and tests. Furthermore, this individual should empower you so that you can rise above your circumstances. This role can be fulfilled by many people. In this chapter, you will find researched based criteria for choosing an ideal support system. Transformational Coaching is presented as an ideal support system that can help you reach your goals and be successful. Four qualities of a Transformational Coaching are presented for you to review. Continuing after that section is a contrastive study on other supportive partnerships that are out there which many people have used.

Towards the end of the chapter you will learn the most effective way to work with your Transformational Coaching or any coach for that matter.

In all ventures, a supportive partnership or support team is very important. Partnerships have always been a huge part of the success story. In past generations and in our current society, partnerships have built many successful enterprises.

Joseph Campbell, with his knowledge of mythology and over-arching ability of story-telling, collaborated with George Lucas to integrate stages of the hero's journey into the Star

Wars saga. What was the final result of this partnership? In October 2012, the Walt Disney Company purchased Lucasfilm for $4.05 billion dollars.

The real power of Transformational Coaching is in the synergy of the partnership. One person cannot do everything. We all need help from others. Frankly, it's hard to imagine any success story without the help of somebody else. As you look for a partnership, consider the following four qualities of a Transformational Coaching :

The First quality of a Transformational Coach is to enable synergy with others.

The real power in any partnership is the collaboration of two people, It's the collaboration they share when working together. To explain this, I have provided an example that shows the interplay of mental functions and how well they can balance each other out.

Here is the real-life example of this kind of **synergy or teamwork** at work, This example is from the book *Pathways to Integrity:*

> Phil Jackson, coach of the Chicago Bulls and the Los Angeles Lakers in the NBA, won six NBA championships with the Bulls and set the standard for excellence in the sport. He went on to become a winner with the Lakers as well. In his book *Sacred Hoops* (1995), Coach Jackson reveals a coaching style that is highly intuitive. While professional coaching has become a scientifically-based numbers game of interchangeable parts in which the head coach is a "control-o-holic" business executive. Jackson's style is that of an artist and shaman. Though all

good coaches use the function of intuition, Jackson is an example of this function, *Par excellence.* He is a maverick in a profession dominated by the style of sensing types.

Jackson contrasts his intuitive style of coaching with the sensing oriented assistant Charley Rosen. Jackson writes: 'Rosen and I were a good match. He saw everything in black and white; I saw infinite graduations of gray. He was obsessed with pinpointing the exact moment when everything turned to crap and who was to blame – more often than not, a referee. I was more interested in the quality of the team's energy as it ebbed and flowed, and figuring out what lessons could be learned when disaster struck. As my wife likes to say, I can smell a rose in a pile of manure' (*Sacred Hoops*, pg. 62). (Quoted from Pathways)

Jackson sees his role as cultivating an atmosphere in which the creative intuition of each player and of the team itself is unleashed during a basketball game. In this atmosphere of trust developed at a "deep level" whereby players know "instinctively how their teammates" will respond in pressure situations (p. 18). For Jackson, being aware of the whole (N)[1] is more important than being fundamentally sound and (focusing on) specific skills of the game (S)[2].

Jackson seeks to balance his approach by hiring assistants (like Charley Rosen or Tex Winters), Sensing types who master and teach the nuts and bolts of component [basketball] skills"
(*Pathways to Integrity*, Blake W. Burleson, p. 30–31)

The key activity in synergy is compensation

As we saw in the previous quote, "Jackson sees his role as cultivating an atmosphere in which the creative intuition of each player and of the team itself is unleashed during a basketball game" Jackson seeks to compensate for what he is not focused on with the help of Charlie Rosen. In this sense, Charlie Rosen was working on more nuts and bolts activities like shooting, and passing, while Jackson focused on big picture concepts. Without forcing Jackson to change, Rosen simply observed what Jackson was doing and tied up the loose ends.

To exemplify this idea in literature, let's consider the classic detective partnership that we see in Sir Arthur Conan Doyle's *Sherlock Homes* series. Here, we are introduced to the partnership between Sherlock Holmes and Dr. Watson.

---

[2] This (S) stands for Sensing. It is referring to the preference of S in the MBTI more information can be found under "The four mental functions" in the next chapter

[1] (N) stands for iNtuition. It refers to the preference of N in MBTI

This is another classic compensatory relationship that is relevant. One is a kind of artist, involved in the world of the arts, and the other is a scientist involved in the world of details and numbers. One uses inductive reasoning, and the other uses deductive reasoning. In this type of mystery/drama investigation, this type of relationship is very useful because the characters complete each other; one sees what the other doesn't.

The challenge in this relationship is that each needs to tolerate the other person's differences. Both need to maximize their strengths so they can solve the mystery and close the case.

This same challenge presents itself and repeats itself in a plethora of examples from television series and movies, such *Castle, White Collar, Men In Black, Rush Hour*, and *Starsky and Hutch*, just to name a few.

Likewise, a Transform Coach offers many forms of compensation to you in the form of balancing, complementing, supplementing and adjusting your viewpoint or approach you are taking. This is in order to help you adapt to new situations, make you more aware of the bigger picture and different variables at play and overall make you more successful.

The second quality of a Transformational Coach : facilitator

A coach facilitates the process of internal compensation within our minds.

Internal compensation as opposed to team compensation works a bit differently. The Transformational Coaching goal is for you to be the captain of your own ship, to empower and provide you with tools and teaching to gain insight into yourself. The master of internal compensation is Carl Jung. In his landmark book, *Psychological Types: the Collected Works of C. G. Jung*, he defines compensation as a supplementing process in your mind and refers to "consciousness" as a selective process in our view of things and the way they appear.

Jung says:

"I conceive it as functional adjustment in general, an inherent self-regulation of the psychic apparatus [the mind] in this sense; I regard the activity of the unconscious as a balancing of the one sidedness of the general attitude produced by the function of consciousness."

He goes on to say..

"Only a limited number of contents can be held in the conscious field at the same time, and of these, only a few can attain the highest grade of consciousness."

This shows that..

The activity of consciousness is *selective*. Selection demands *direction*. But direction requires the *exclusion of everything irrelevant*. This is bound to make a conscious *orientation* one-sided. The contents that are excluded and inhibited by the chosen direction sink into the unconscious, where they form a counterweight to the conscious *orientation*. The strengthening of this counter position keeps pace with the increase of conscious one sidedness until finally a noticeable tension is produced...."

So in essence there can be something we keep putting off and putting off. It could be taking a vacation, it could be a conversation with your significant other about something you want to say but don't want to hurt their feelings in saying.

It could be that you have forgotten a special date, because you were so focused on hitting a particular deadline or completing a particular project at work.

This one-sided attitude can easily be seen in the way google is giving us information more and more, Through machine learning it starts to know our viewpoints and our conscious orientation to seeing the world. It then sends out information to prove our viewpoints right. This again is a problem because focused on one puzzle piece you miss out on the big picture.

When Jung speaks of this, I cannot help to think of the classic Ego vs. Shadow relationship that Jung is known for.

If your way of being, is constantly nice, pleasant, don't won't to rock the boat, to the point where you are spineless and people walk all over you. You are too far on the one way of being.

As Jung says "The more one- sided the conscious attitude, the more antagonistic the contents are arising from the unconscious"

This is to say the "Shadow" which is the opposite of your conscious orientation (spineless and people walk all over you) comes out in a upwelling of anger to control and have your way, strictly, forcefully and in exact accord with what you said.

(*Psychological Types* by C. G. Jung, p. 419)

Because of this phenomenon, we can't speak in a positive and negative way at the same time. If we do, it will be confusing and unclear. This concept of being "one-sided" is a big one! When we fail to see the other side we often make impulsive decisions to our determent. Seeking the middle way is not often easy. Your coach or counselor can help you with this. I have made an illustration to further explain taking the middle way.

The goal in life is to take the middle way.

To further illustrate how this adjusting, supplementing and balancing works, consider the following graphic below about the Head vs. Heart or Thinking vs Feeling. (Figure 9)

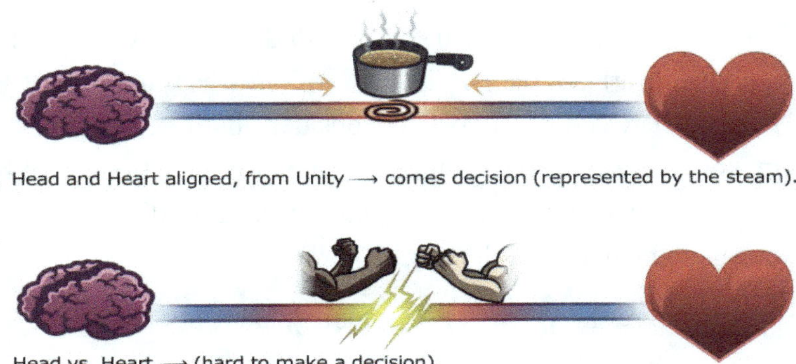

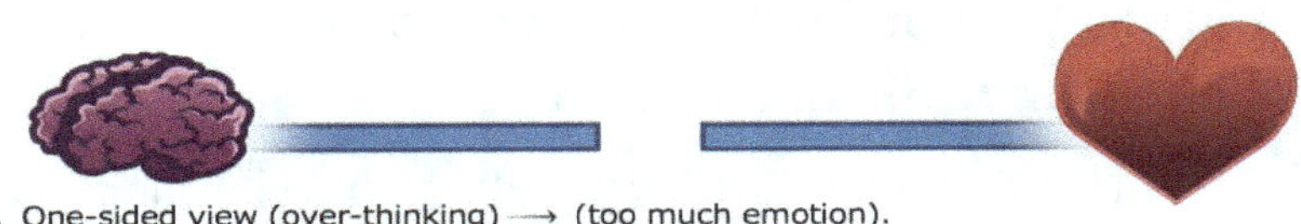

Figure 9

When approaching a problem, some people see only a one-sided view, illustrated as C in the graph. A one-sided view means that you only use your head (over thinking, analyzing logically) to solve problems or you only use your heart (too much emotion).

Others, as in example B, have head and heart in opposition. They are in a struggle and can't see a way out. One side may win and the other may lose. Or it could be a draw, with no decision made.

Few understand that there is a midpoint between the head and the heart as seen in part A of the diagram. There is a balance between the two that considers both perspectives and makes a conscious decision in the face of both options once they are both presented. This new attitude or condition is what it means to take the middle way.

We live in a world of duality and at times we lose perspective and forget there is a middle way.

Finding the middle way with your Transformational Coach

Using the process Jung called Individuation; your Transformational Coach will help you find the right solution, for the challenges in your life. In association with Individuation the transcendent function plays a huge part. It is the function that enables a transition from one attitude or condition to another. Whenever your conscious mind is engaged between heart vs. mind, two seemingly opposite symbols, a noticeable tension is produced. The transcendent function has a healing effect by creating unity and bridging a gap between the two. Moving beyond one-sidedness and allowing you to feel whole. This type of thinking with your Transformational coach can free you to make choices, help you bring up all unconscious (unaware) possibilities that have developed in you, and then help you to make a sound decision in the face of all other options. It's like having a table of Lego pieces and picking the one piece that will fit into your life story.

Conclusions drawn from the centered view or middle way result in less nervousness and anxiety.

If one-sidedness causes anxiety, why do we use it?

When you are working really hard on something, you tend to put blinders on and focus only on that task at hand. Those blinders, although needed, can cause you to overlook some minor details and ultimately lose out on some big opportunities. Not seeing the bigger picture could cost you what is called the "opportunity cost," and "relationship cost," the cost of losing out on a valuable relationship or opportunity.

So, ask yourself this: if something is blinding you on the path to being a complete success, when would you want to know about it? When it is easy to prepare for? Or when it's already over and difficult to recover? The answer is obvious: it's easier when we think proactively.

Sun Tzu a revered military strategist author of the book, *The Art of War* which ultimately practices a way of winning before fighting, applies this same proactive strategy to his warriors of ancient times. Let's read how he did this:

> Plan for what is difficult while it is easy, do what is great while it is small. The most difficult things in the world must be done while they are still easy, the greatest things in the world must be

done while they are still small. For this reason sages never do what is great, and this is why they can achieve that greatness. *(The Art of War,* Sun Tzu, p.2)

Essentially what we are reading about here is being proactive and planning your future moves with the big picture in mind. Like Sherlock Holmes and Dr. Watson solving mysteries, your Transformational Coach will help you discover and seek out the answers to the mysteries in your life. Help you to see clearly what you really want out of it and reveal any unintended consequences. He or she will help you uncover any potential opportunities for career advancement, personal growth, new relationships, and overall success. Having this time to reflect with all the information in front of you, not only leads to better decisions but also allows you to clarify what really matters then pursue those wants and needs to the best of your ability.

The third quality: A Transformational Coach is a manager without being your boss

In my training and experience in talking with clients and people who have been coached, most have said that accountability is a very important part of the coaching process.

Simply having someone to talk to, someone to be your springboard for thoughts and ideas is vital. It is best to connect with someone who is open to what you have to say, someone who is interested, imaginative, innovative, accepting, and nonjudgmental, this process is 100% focused on you.

Most of us are familiar with accountability, at home, your

mom tells you to pick up your clothes off the floor or clean up the kitchen when you are done with. At work, your manager has a quota for you hit every month and they are on your back about it. Some people like micro-managing but most of us don't. The way a Transformational Coach fulfills the duty of being a manager is quite different than the way you may be accustomed to seeing. To further explain let's take a look at a typical performance review in corporate America.

Stephan Kraus speaks about an annual performance review that focuses more on weakness then strengths:

> Let's consider the typical hour-long annual performance review. A manager sits down with his/her employee and spends the first two minutes praising the employee's strengths and accomplishments. Then, the manager spends fifty-six minutes harping on the employee's failures and weaknesses. We live in a politically correct society, and as such, they are labeled, 'opportunities for improvement', 'areas of growth' or 'deltas', but we all know what the manager really means: *Weaknesses*. In the final four minutes of the review, the manager spells out the employee's goals and objectives for the coming year. In an effort to create balance and well-rounded employees, those goals invariably ignore strengths and focus on improving weaknesses. In fact, advancement and promotion are generally tied to improving a weakness to an adequate level. (*Psychological Foundations of Success*, Stephen J. Kraus, p. 88)

A Transformational Coach, on the other hand, will not follow this pattern. He will **co-create the coaching relationship** with and use a form of accountability that is tailor-fit for you. Your strengths and your skill sets. He or she will help you maximize your strengths, put you where you can do your personal best, and find immediate success.

The fourth quality: A Transformational Coach is a teacher and strategist

Just as a teacher helps you to learn about facts and concepts in school, a Transformational Coach helps you learn about the project or journey you're entering. Your Transformational Coach helps you stand back, become more aware of the bigger picture. They help you see things from a higher vantage point. Your coach will enable you to be more prepared for all and any unintended consequences. This allows you to capitalize on opportunities that may come your way, especially if you are figuring something out for the first time and strategizing your best course of action. Discussing the options with your Transformational Coach will help you learn something new every time and help you see your situation from different perspectives. Such guidance will help you find a way that works for you. This will maximize your time, effort, and strengths.

Who benefits most from Transformational Coaching?

The beneficiaries of Transformational Coaching are directors, entrepreneurs, innovators, inventors and many others mentioned in the introduction. Typically, anyone seeking to improve and follow their dreams. These tend to be people that have ambitions, dreams, and visions and want to do something about them. Yet Transformational Coaching also applies to any business owner or educator who wants to achieve more success in the career of their choosing—to be more productive. This is because Transformational Coaching strives to be like a turbo-charger for an engine. The engine can run on its own, but with a turbo-charger added, its power is enhanced.

In this new digital age, different types of media, pictures, videos, music, and eBooks can be sent instantly to anywhere and picked up by anyone; your voice can be heard across the world. Processes that once took months or years can be fully automated and fly through cyberspace to be shared and distributed almost instantly.

In fact, there is so much technology available now that it's sometimes difficult to keep up with it all. It can be overwhelming and overreaching at times. Rather than empowering you, you may become a victim of it.

We live in a world that keeps us unequal. Technology is probably the greatest benefit of living in the developed world, and it can definitely improve our lives, yet the majority of us are not aware of its potential and may not even be using it. without a coach, one of our greatest resources remains untapped.

With your Transformational Coach, you can discover how to tap into great resources and powerful technologies and learn how to get them to work for you. They can free up your time and automate many of today's processes. Ultimately, we will apply them to an action plan created for you to integrate all the steps necessary for your success effectively.

Co-creating the Coaching Relationship

Co-creating relates to how you will help yourself, and how your Transformational Coach will help you to help yourself. The coaching relationship is a designed alliance to help you achieve your goals. It is important to ask for what you need from a Transformational Coach (within reason), to help you achieve your goals.

You may have many questions for your coach. What are the time constraints? When can we best work together? How often would it be? A Transformational Coach is someone who sits outside your social setting and comes into your life at pre- determined intervals.

With regard to work and family life, your Coach obviously doesn't want to disturb or disrupt it. It is your duty to find the time (at predetermined intervals) to meet as often as needed. Coaching sessions should not conflict with your work or family life.

It's also important to be truthful and honest with yourself regarding your needs and wants from the coaching partnership. Together, you and your Transformational coach will discover how we can best work to meet these needs.

You must already have a sense of self-caring, self-responsibility, and self-reliance because your Transformational coach is not going to actually do a project for you. Your Transformational coach assists in the process. A key part of the coaching process is asking for what you need so the coach knows how to help you.

An individual must nurture or love his or her own self before he or she can have someone else be nurturing. Giving an individual personal space and autonomy is the best way for an individual to care for themselves.

When a Transformational Coach brings clients to the optimal level, it is like eating nutritious food for the body. It's a choice to do better for your mind and body, to energize you and to bring you to a super-charged level.

We live in a rapidly changing society, and we are moving at an unnaturally fast speed every day. It's very difficult to keep up unless we delegate responsibilities and share the load of our lofty ambitions with a Transformational coach.

The role of the Coach is to feed you healthy and nutritious food for thought and supply a fertile ground of nutritious soil for your ambitions and ideas to grow. Through diligent efforts, we work together and strive to connect your ideas with action goals.

The Courage to Ask for What You Need

Lastly, when working with a coach the most important thing to remember is **to ask for what you need,** and stay grounded in that.

It is important to point out the struggle in **asking for what you need**. This is important in order to provide you with the best guidance and awareness of the roadblocks in your life, so you can be alert and ready for them when they come up.

To give an example, let's consider a person on a vegan diet. This is a diet that is difficult to maintain in a world where meat and dairy products are the norm and few exceptions are available. Vegans must continually ask for what they need; otherwise, they will not receive it. As their needs become more pronounced, more products are likely to appear. This is also true of those that are gluten sensitive. They need to seek out and ask for products that they can eat. There is a big movement now to produce these products because people have been vocal about asking for what they need.

But, this concept of asking for you what you need is deeper than this. It also found in the book *Outliers* by Malcom Gladwell, specifically the chapter "The trouble with geniuses, part 2" in the pages 101 to 108. There is a great study cited by the sociologist Annette Lareau on a group of third graders. Gladwell explains the study in more detail in his book. "She picked both blacks and whites and children from wealthy homes and poor homes, zeroing in,

ultimately, on twelve families. Lareau and her team visited each family at least twenty times, for hours at a stretch."

To give additional information about Annette Lareau in her book, Unequal Childhoods, she explains that people don't ask for what they need because of the way they were raised; this starts from a young age. What I am talking about here are parenting styles that produce a specific type of attitude and skill. According to Annette Lareau there are two parenting styles, concerted cultivation, and natural growth. The middle class or wealthy follows concerted cultivation and the working class or poorer follow natural growth.

Going back to Gladwell, he goes on to say "Lareau

stresses that one style isn't morally better than the other. The poorer children were, to her mind, often better behaved, less whiny, more creative in making use of their own time, and had a well-developed sense of independence." (Pg. 104)

Middle-class parents who comply with current professional standards and engage in a pattern of "concerted cultivation" deliberately try to stimulate their children's development and foster their cognitive and social skills. Because of this, from a young age they were taught to speak up and ask the person in authority for what they want or need, be it a doctor, karate instructor, etc.

Others that followed the path of natural growth were not as "entitled" financially, so they didn't have those experiences. Because of this they didn't feel like they had the right to ask for what they want or need, likely because they have not been through a "concerted cultivation" process from a young age. So they didn't build those social skills. They

were not expected to talk back to their parents, to negotiate or to question adults in positions of authority.

"In Lareau's words, the middle-class children learn a sense of entitlement. That word, of course, has negative connotations these days. But Lareau means it in the best sense of the term:

> They acted as though they had a right to pursue their own individual preferences and to actively manage interactions in institutional settings. They appeared comfortable in those settings; they were open to sharing information and asking for attention...it was common practice among middle class children to shift

interactions to suit their **preferences.**" [bold added] (*Outliers,* Malcom Gladwell, p. 105)

The sense of entitlement that has been taught to them is an attitude perfectly suited to succeeding in the modern world. The individual should ask for what they need to succeed, speak up in social situations, reason, negotiate, be assertive, and make jokes when appropriate.

Asking for what you need takes courage. What some people need is courage, and self-confidence. If they were not brought up with it or did not develop that character trait during the course of their upbringing then they will need help to develop it, become accustomed to using it and be able to benefit from it. This is where a Transformational Coach can come in. Through the partnership and coaching sessions, the person can be lead to believe in themselves again, develop more boldness, and use their strengths to achieve what they want to achieve. Therefore, a person can be encouraged to stand on their own two feet and face challenges without backing down, no matter what.

In conclusion, this kind of guidance along with a solid action plan (previously mentioned as a mind map) is exactly what a Transformational Coach has to offer you. Couple this with your willingness to persevere though obstacles, and anything is achievable.

Now that you have read both Chapter three and Chapter four.

It's time to take out a journal and write out what helped you most .

In chapter three, how are your listening skills and how does it match up with the kind of listening illustrated in the image.

What areas of life are you least clear on and would like clarity?

In Chapter four,
How will you navigate this "special world" Who will be your guide?

You will need someone to help you discern between who are your enemies and who are your allies.. who will that be?

Stage Two: Revealing the "authentic you": Individuality and character development

The self is infinite and full of untapped potential; it contains all the unconscious aspects of the psyche and the conscious aspects of it too.

This chapter marks the transition from the ordinary world into the special world. The upcoming chapters 5-8 cover steps 5-9 in the hero's journey. If you re-call Steps 5 through 9 are aligned with your private and individual journey, the journey only you fully know. It is also the called a "soul journey," where you find out more about yourself and push your limits. **It is where you turn inward to explore, reflect, fight the dragons, claim your gifts, and discover your strengths and talents.**

Exploring the idea of Your Independent Spirit and Individuality

Individual spirit is special because it is where we get our originality, inventiveness, and creativity. Sometimes it is neglected and hidden behind the mask we wear for society. This is to say that the persona or mask becomes thick. When this happens, you really need to start excavating to break through that persona. It's just a smoke screen, and should be temporary. What you need to do is recapture your individual spirit. Like a rare and precious mineral beneath bedrock, it takes some time and trouble to separate the individual spirit from the persona; it takes careful mining and digging within you to find each jewel in its own right.

Overall it's very important to study yourself, and to live as genuinely and authentically as you can.

Jung explains:

> In this generation–and in those to come–it is very important that we continue the individual work of self-discovery and not abandon needed psychological reflection for the easy ephemera of mass culture. Only individual awareness of both the conscious and unconscious aspects of the human psyche will allow the great work of human culture to continue and thrive. *(The Undiscovered Self, C.G. Jung, back cover)*

"The easy ephemera of mass culture" means things that are short-lived and popular for the present moment, until something better comes along. Like the fleeting "celebrities" of the *Jersey Shore*, or *The Real Housewives of Your Nearby City*, their celebrity status is typically short-lived.

Let's go a little deeper. Let's say you choose to identify yourself with such ephemera and not with your individual spirit. In that case, your spirt will only be aligned with something that is temporary and manufactured by TV or a societal mask that we just were for others. Well, this is just a persona; it's a temporary thing, never let the mask be greater than the "self" or let the "self" be contained only to the persona. ***The "self" is infinite*** and full of untapped potential; it contains all the unconscious aspects of the psyche and the conscious aspects of it too.

There is a saying in Zen Buddhism: always seek to mesh the present with the eternal. The present which is temporary, is what's happening ***now*** in your life, the eternal is your entire life and your legacy. Once you realize this you will find that your future is a consequence of what you are doing now. Seek to take action in such a way that your effort lasts through time. Like a book that takes five years to write but lasts a lifetime, or a movie like "The Wizard of OZ" "Gone with the Wind" or "Citizen Kane."

This temporal thing is just a test; there will be more to come, so keep your vision clear and the big picture in mind, like Dorothy's yellow brick road, your mind-map keeps you on track. What you do today echoes into eternity.

Don't give up on excavating the authentic you. It is a privilege to be unique, a special right granted to those who have gone through the psychological development to get there.

The psychological development underlying being unique is the process of individuation. This is defined in the following two quotes, and defined more extensively in the third.

> The concept of individuation plays a very large role in our (Jungian) psychology. In general, it is the process which individual beings are formed and differentiated (*Psychological Types* by C. G. Jung, p. 448)

The process of self-development in which an individual integrates the many facets of the psyche to become him or her*self*... (From *Introducing Jung* by Maggie Hyde and Michael McGuinness, p.173).

In particular, it is the development of the psychological *individual* as being distinct from the general, collective psychology. Individuation therefore is a process of *differentiation* having for its goal the development of the individual personality. Individuation is a natural necessity inasmuch as its prevention by leveling down to collective standards is injurious to the vital activity of the individual.

Individuation is always to some extent opposed to collective norms, since it means separation and differentiation from the general and a building up of the particular [individual].

Under no circumstances can individuation be the sole aim of psychological education. Before it can be taken as a goal, the education aim of adaptation to the necessary minimum of collective norms must first be attained. (*Psychological Types* by C. G. Jung, p. 449)

Overall, individuation is about reaching your full potential and achieving psychic wholeness. Dignity and stability are also marks of the unique or individual personality, as are respect and acceptance for oneself and others' personal growth. Those who reach individuation bear in mind that each individual can be different but still be alike. Becoming more tolerable of others, and being more of a global citizen.

If you have gone through this psychological development, you can more freely and independently think and not blindly obey what society wants you to be right now. You do things consciously because you *want to*. It aligns with who you are, your values, and the goals you have.

If you haven't gone through this psychological development.. Your assignment is to realize and clarify the person you want to be, not what your friends want you to be, not what your company wants you to be, and not what America wants you to be. Who do *you* want to be?

Collective norms, now a day seems to be led by consumerism or the media and their propaganda. Consider these words:

> "Two generations of American's have grown up in the television age, during which consumerism has achieved unprecedented dominance over our value system…. our society is now organized around an economic system that seemingly demands a continuing high level of consumer spending." *(Mastery,* George Leonard, p. 30)

Leonard's words were from 1992; nearly 30 years later and nothing has changed. 2016 and nothing has changed. Through television, in-print and radio commercials and advertisements, we have lost our value selection process and given up to consumerism.

We have become a throwaway society with an attitude of "it's replaceable—I can just buy a new one!" We don't find value in what we have; we just throw it away like plastic bottles and get new one.

By extension, the danger with this philosophy is that we as people disregard our value. Abandoning our own values for the values of society in today's day is dangerous. The type of person that Capitalism and Consumerism creates is a person obsessed with extrinsic goals such as, money, image, and status. Superficial traps such as power, material wealth and fame.

All is not negative however. There is a benefit to all this growth America is having.

Naomi L. Quenk offers these words:

> Civilization's advancement has been marked by increasing specialization in the knowledge and skills required for human survival and progress and people in this modern civilization are ill equipped to exist on their own in this increasingly complex world without these people that have specialized. So we have become highly specialized or differentiated in our knowledge and skills, and therefore require a very large and complex society to meet our survival and progressive needs. Our increasing differentiation as individuals has led to our ability to significantly affect our environment… (Naomi L. Quenk. *Was that Really Me?* p. 23)

So the ever-increasing specialization associated with our civilization means that if you are unique, different, and have something to offer to society that is uniquely yours, you could make big money!!! You could rise up the ranks quite quickly. You just need to have the correct leadership skills and VALUES in place.

A good example of companies that made big money and rose up the ranks quickly for being special and thinking differently are the entrepreneurs that created Netflix, Uber, Air B&B, GotoMeeting, Alibaba.com, and Salesforce. All of these businesses were started by people who had a **vision**. The creators or founders of these companies were foreseeing the needs of society in North America and created a masterful product to go along with it. The above businesses were able to create a product that was original, inventive, creative and just what they envisioned people would want. What made them famous was how they brought the vision to action.

What is harder to understand is the values they had in their hearts when trying to build this company and how they actually did it, unless they write a book about it or a documentary . Many do!

You have to ask yourself, if I were to emulate them in a productive way and pull out a skeletal system, what would it look like? I believe it would be the same values Jeff Nelson, the CEO of OneGoal encourages its teachers to have as "Leadership Principles." In Paul Tough's book, *How Children Succeed,* he explains what these principles are….

"Nelson, using instinct more than research, identified five skills, which he called leadership principles, that he wanted OneGoal teachers to emphasize: **resourcefulness, resilience, ambition, professionalism and integrity.** Those words now permeate the program" [bold added] (p. 162)

I believe all the previously mentioned companies and founders have incorporated the leadership principles mentioned in this quote. That is why they have been successful.

Lastly, I would like to wrap this chapter up by referencing the "return" section in the Hero's Journey from Joseph Campbell's book, *Reflections on the Art of Living*. Here he has some final words about bringing your vision into action. (p. 80 – 81)

"An image of the return that amuses me is that of a young man who comes from Wisconsin to New York to study art. He's gone into Greenwich Village, the underworld of Manhattan. He has to help him… a master who he is studying. He finally achieves an art style. Then, having achieved his style, he comes to 57th Street with his paintings and meets the cold eye of the dealer.

The great problem is bringing life back
into the wasteland, where people live inauthentically.

Bringing back the gift to integrate it into a rational life is very difficult. It is even more difficult than going down into the underworld [special world] to get it. What you have to bring back is something that the world lacks----which is why you went to get it----and lacking it, the world does not know that it needs it. So, on your return, when you come with your boon [vision] for the world and there is no reception, what are you going to do?" (p. 80 – 81)

Campbell continues to give advice as to how to tackle this in the coming pages of his book, you will have to read his book to get more of it. For our purposes, I will just quote a portion of what he says; "You try to find a means to deliver what you have found as the life boon [your gifts, special talents or product you discovered] in terms and in the proportions that are proper to the world's ability to receive. It takes a good deal of compassion and patience." (p. 81-82) [comment added]

Lastly, DON'T GIVE UP! KEEP FIGHTING!

Keep going on until you are a success!

C H A P T E R 6

Theory Behind Personality Assessments

Going with your natural tendencies leads to working little and producing great results. Going against your natural tendencies leads to working too hard to produce too little.

This chapter aims to assist you in the recognizing of your own strengths and is a further step to the revealing of the authentic you. This is done by presenting the theory of psychological types, and the instrument that was made to assess it, the Myers-Briggs Type Indicator (MBTI). Then it goes into speaking about type dynamics, including mental function pairs. After that, David Kerisey's temperament theory is presented from his book "Please Understand me II, temperament character intelligence" In which he builds off the Myers-Briggs theory but speaks of intelligence roles instead of psychological types and cites his difference. David Kerisey gives each type a name and really goes in-depth into what each type would value, their vocational interest, leadership style and much more. He also has an assessment called the Keirsey temperament sorter II (KTS II)

In the hero's Journey this can be connected to Step six – "the approach to the innermost cave"

Lastly, I have added Kathy Kolbe's theory on Instincts as presented in her book the *Conative Connection* and *Powered by Instinct.* She has an assessment you can take called the Kolbe A Index. These were all picked for a variety of reasons. First off, these personality assessments are all valid and reliable from a statistics standpoint and have years of experience behind it. This is unlike, horoscopes, color tests and things of that nature.

The proceeding is background information on the theory of psychological types and how it works, this passage is from the back cover of Psychological Types.

"He [Jung] called it the fruit of nearly twenty years' work in the domain of practical psychology and In his autobiography he [Jung] wrote:

> This work sprang originally from my need to define the ways in which my outlook differed from Freud's and Adler's. In attempting to answer this question, I came across the problem of types; for it is one's psychological type which from the outset determines and limits a person's judgment. My book, therefore, was an effort to deal with the relationship of the individual to the world, to people and things. I discussed the various aspects of consciousness, the various attitudes the conscious mind might take toward the world, and thus constitutes a psychology of

Stage Two: Revealing the authentic you
consciousness regarded from what might be called a clinical angle. (*Psychological Types* by C. G. Jung)

A psychological type is a kind of mentality we hold on to. It can be likened to a lens through which we see life. The theory first arose in 1923 and is still used today. It has stood the test of time.

One of the most important facts about type theory and all the theory's explained in this chapter is that it describes each personality as *healthy, adapted, and of equal inherent value.*

Type descriptions emphasize the positive attributes of each type. In fact, a significant asset of this approach compared to pathology-focused systems that focus on disorder and disease is its validating and affirming nature. It empowers you to be courageously confident in *who* you are!

The Myers-Briggs Type Indicator-An instrument to determine the "Authentic You."

Knowing your personality type can help you be:

- More responsible to yourself, to others, and to institutions
- More independent and free
- More conscious and in control of your life
- More connected, real, and authentic
  (Back Cover, *The sixteen personality types*, L. Berens and D. Nardi)

A very commonly used assessment for self-reflection and self-understanding is the *Myers-Briggs Type Indicator* (MBTI). Using the MBTI, people find out what personality type they are. The instrument determines your type code and your answers reveal your personality tendencies. The following is an explanation from the MBTI manual:

> "The purpose of the Myers-Briggs Type Indicator® (MBTI®) personality inventory is to make the theory of psychological types described by C. G. Jung understandable and useful in people's lives. The essence of the theory is that
>
> much seemingly random variation in the behavior is actually quite orderly and consistent, being due to basic differences in the ways individuals prefer to use their perception and judgment.
>
> Perception involves all the ways of becoming aware of things, people, happenings, or ideas. Judgment involves all the ways of coming to conclusions about what has been perceived. If people differ systematically in what they perceive and in how they reach conclusions, then it is only reasonable for them to differ correspondingly in their interests, reactions, values, motivations, and skills" (MBTI manual, third edition)

According to type theory, people create their own type by constantly choosing to exercise a certain way of perceiving information known in the MBTI as Sensing or Intuition. Then, they make a judgment on this information using what is known in the MBTI as either Thinking or Feeling. When one perception and one judgment are combined, they make a function pair or what is called a "cognitive core" of the personality. Let's take sensing and thinking (ST) for example: it means taking the perception of sensing, which is a practical, common sense perception and applying it in a logical, analytical way. It is said that the person is naturally attracted to this certain way of perceiving information and a certain way of making a judgment on this information (that is, it is innate, inborn, and natural).

As noted, people create their own type by constantly choosing to exercise a certain way of perceiving information and then making a judgment on that information. The interests, values, needs, and habits of that kind of person naturally blend together and produce a kind of outline or type code such as "ISTJ" to create a general outline of what perceptions and judgements that person is going to favor. An outline is precisely what the system of typology offers.

This is important because we all have habits which translate to certain natural strengths and learned behaviors. There are things we are naturally good at (strengths) and things we are taught how to be good at (learned strengths). Beyond this, there is another distinction to be made. This distinction is between personal strengths and advantages that we have in life. The ability to separate personal strengths from advantages and learned behaviors is vital. If you don't separate them, you may end up wasting time on the wrong things.

Here are some examples: having a flashy new car, the latest fashionable shoes, a higher education degree like an MBA or PhD, a million-dollar inheritance, or even the latest in technology is an advantage. These are material possessions or titles that could get your foot in the door or make it easier to get around and do certain things. But, relying on them too heavily can be a problem. These are external advantages. You need to rely more on your internal strengths. This is explained in the following quote from *Soar with your Strengths* by Donald O. Clifton and Paula Nelson; "A strength is an inner ability, something that can be displayed in a performance, verses a material possession or title." They can be such things like, being courageous, having a sense of humor, having an imagination, and being genuinely friendly.

To be inventive and having the knack for creating things, (like the latest technology) is a strength. So, look inside yourself for value and wealth instead of outside at material possessions, and you will find that inside of you is a boundless treasure chest overflowing with immeasurable gold, *this* is the **true human resource.**

Walk instead on your own two feet and trust in your personality strengths. A bird sitting on a tree is never afraid of the branch breaking, because its trust is not on the branch but on its own wings. Always believe in yourself!

With the right person to administer, interpret, and apply findings, an individual can accurately predict what this type might be, drawing from ideas firmly based on the dynamics of type theory, years of observation of the types, and empirical results from research.

It is important to note that the MBTI type does not lead to stereotyping or pigeon-holing. We can reasonably expect a person with an outline or (type code) to be different from others in ways characteristic of a previously known type codes.

To describe a person as belonging to a type (if they agree a certain combination is their type) in no way infringes on their right to be who they want to be.

These are not unbreakable rules, and you can draw outside of the lines. They are intended only to guide you. People of the same type can be quite different. The MBTI type is just one facet of that person; it only describes them in part. Ultimately, you define who you are in each moment with the choices you make. No one has made exactly the

same choices as you have. This makes your life unique. It also makes your strengths sacred, as no one has made every single choice exactly the same as you have. In other words, because of the path you have taken in your life, your strengths remain sacred. We are now the printout or the product of many, many, many choices in life, be they intentional or unintentional.

In type code, the first letter (whether it be E or I) speaks of the dichotomy of Extravert and Introvert, This dichotomy is essentially about **psychological energy.**

What Is Psychological Energy?

Psychological energy is simply mental energy. In this context it's best to think of Introversion and Extroversion as verbs, it is something we do. Constantly choosing the one that is not your preference can lead you to mental exhaustion.

This idea is simple, Extroverts like to talk and be out and about doing things, lots of various things and activities. These are preferred activities that will stimulate their thoughts and feelings of excitement, pleasure, and well-being.

Conversely, if extroverts are doing activities introverts usually enjoy like staying at home and reading a book or going deeply into a specific topic or activity. This can reduce or deplete thoughts and feelings of excitement, pleasure, and well- being for extroverts.

During these non-preferred activities over a long period of time for extroverts can actually result in a sense of frustration, boredom, irritation, and mental exhaustion.

For example, staying indoors on a rainy day reading a book or quietly doing a craft may give great joy and peace to introverts who prefer acquiring and distributing energy internally. Yet, this may (after a short time) leave extraverts bored. They need to go somewhere to interact more directly and physically with individuals or the environment.

It is my perception that "introvert" has a bad reputation in society; I have heard some people describe a introvert being perceived as shy, timid, and maybe even awkward. It's as if no one wants to be called an introvert. As if it's a negative term. And, if these qualities were universally true, then throw away all the television shows, all the movies, all the great dramas, and all the great plays you have enjoyed over the years, because all these started with great writers— mostly introverts. Their role is reflective, and they definitely enjoy being behind the scenes more than extroverts. But to not recognize the great talent that introverts provide is to deny the most fundamental function of any popular media. All we see are the actors in their expressive roles, acting out what was written behind the scenes.

The writers, like most introverts, are usually working in private or by themselves, reflecting inwardly more than they express externally. So, the social perceptions of the term are false.

The term "introvert" simply means more reflective then expressive compared to extraverts (who will say just about everything and anything, whether solicited or unsolicited). This is a very important function in society. People have preferences. The introvert prefers to recharge his or her energy by doing quieter things such as reading a book, doing a craft, or doing something with their energy focused more internally. Extraverts, in contrast, gain energy and recharge their batteries by socializing with friends.

When psychological energy drops, the experience is the same for those preferring extraversion or introversion. It is lower mood, boredom, irritability, and frustration. This means that emotional and mental engagement is falling or being reduced. It can even mean disengagement. This is something you want to avoid if you are working with others in a classroom or a boardroom. But it could also be something to keep in mind during family table conversation or with a significant other. Some activities that would increase engagement and psychological energy for those preferring extraversion are involvement in lively company, an interactive presentation, or other social opportunities. This may result in a need to be quiet or alone for individuals preferring introversion. For example, with a presentation, introverts would rather read about the content being presented, which provides the opportunity for reflection and processing in their preferred way.

Now, both introverts and extraverts have advantages. There is an *introvert advantage* (not incidentally also the name of a book by Marti Olsen Laney) and an *extravert advantage*.

The introvert's advantage comes in the form of *depth*. They may have a lack of personal relationships, and they may have fewer interests then the extraverts, but they are laser-focused on the things that interest them. Therefore in the field of their choosing, their activity gains much more depth and their work has a lasting value and impact.

The extravert's advantage comes in the form of *breadth*. They have a lot of interests, personal relationships, and hobbies; as a result, they cast a wide net, gathering all types of information and meeting many people. In this way, many valuable relationships are built up quickly to enrich their work and give it *breadth*. According to Jung: "…both types are capable of enthusiasm, what fills the extravert's heart flows out of his mouth, but the enthusiasm of the introvert is the very thing that seals his lips. He kindles no flame in others and so he lacks colleagues of equal caliber" (*Psychological Types*, C. G. Jung, p. 326)

The introvert and extraverts have a compensatory relationship, which provides both conflict and collaboration; consider the idea of reaction time between the two types to explain their difference.

In a student and teacher relationship, an extraverted teacher will respond quickly to student's question and connect with their need to know with the right words, empathizing with the student the whole time.

On the other hand, an introverted teacher will not react in an instant, but only after a time. They would promise to think it over and after a few days would bring the student the answer. This is not because the introverted thinking was too slow, but because he couldn't comprehend the full impact of the question at the moment.

Although the teacher seemed to react slowly to the student's question, in the book *Psychological Types*, Jung provides a better explanation:

> He merely reacted inwardly rather than outwardly. He did not empathize his student and so did not understand what he needed. His attitude was entirely directed to his own thoughts; consequently, he reacted not to the personal needs of the student but to the thoughts which the question had aroused in himself ... (C. G. Jung, p. 327)

Jung's final words on this are:

> The introvert's attitude is an abstracting one; it is always intent on withdrawing libido (psychic/mental energy) from the object, (object of his affection or thinking could be a person or thing) as though the introvert had to prevent the object from gaining power over him or her.

> The extraverts on the contrary has a positive relation with the object. He affirms its importance to such an extent that his subjective attitude is constantly related to it and oriented by the object. The object can never have enough value for him, and its importance must always be increased. (C. G. Jung, p. 330)

Withdrawing psychic energy as introverts do provides objectivity and leads to *detached involvement*. Pouring in endless amounts of psychic energy as extraverts do provides subjectivity (like taking steps forward to understand the other's point of view) and leads to *attached involvement*. Jung states that "These two types are so different and present such a striking contrast that their existence becomes quite obvious even to the layman once it has been pointed out." (C. G. Jung, Psychological types p. 330)

> Jung concluded that the two types couldn't be "…a matter of conscious judgment or conscious intention but must be due to some unconscious, instinctive cause…(with) some kind of biological foundation" (*Psychological Types*, C. G. Jung, 1990)

About 70 years after publishing *Psychological Types*, scientists can now actually see the difference in the brain between introverts and extraverts: Jung's premise was indeed validated. Brain researchers have identified several physiological differences in the brain that separates extraverts from introverts. "Specifically, one difference is found in the thalamus area and another in the frontal lobes" (from "Cerebral Blood Flow and Personality," *The American Journal of Psychiatry*, pgs. 252-257).

Among all the personality theories in the world, Carl Jung's theory of psychological types has been the most researched and connected to the brain's actual functioning. This is evidenced in various books, including *The Creative Brain* by Ned Herrmann, *Dichotomies of the Mind* by Walter Lowen, *Neuroscience of Personality* by Dario Nardi, and many more.

The Four Mental Functions

The next step in understanding psychological type is to understand the four mental functions. The first two are perception-based, Sensing (S) and Intuition (N) and the second two are judgment-based, Thinking (T) and Feeling (F).

Isabel Briggs Myers and Mary H. McCaulley described the four mental functions in *Pathways to Integrity* by Blake W. Burleson.

They describe the *sensing* function as follows:

> …observable by the way of the senses. Sensing establishes what exists. Because the senses can bring to awareness only what is occurring in the present moment, persons oriented toward sensing perceptions tend to focus on immediate experience available to their five senses. They, therefore, often develop characteristics associated with this awareness such as enjoying the present moment, realism, acute powers of observation, memory for details, and practicality (p. 23).

The *intuition* function is described as the:

> …perception of possibilities, meanings, and relationships by way of insight. Jung characterized intuition as perception by way of the unconscious. intuitions may come to the surface of consciousness suddenly, as a "hunch," the sudden perception of a pattern in seemingly unrelated events. Intuition permits perception beyond what is visible to the senses, including possible future events. People who prefer intuition may develop characteristics that can follow from emphasis on intuition and become imaginative, theoretical, abstract, future-oriented, or creative. Persons oriented towards intuition may also become so intent on pursuing possibilities that they may overlook actualities…

When the sensing function is used to perceive an apple, a person might describe it as juicy, crisp red, or white with black seeds. When intuitive function is used to perceive the same apple, a person may say 'William Tell', 'how to keep the doctor away', 'roast pig', or 'my grandmother's famous pie'. With sensing, we can get a 'factual readout'. With intuition a 'vision of its potential' (pgs.23–24).

The *Thinking* and *Feeling* functions are discriminating and evaluative functions. One uses the head; the other uses the heart.

Myers and McCaulley described *Thinking* as:

…the function that comes to a decision by linking ideas together through logical connections. Thinking relies on principles of cause and effect and tends to be objective and impersonal in the application of reason to a decision. Persons who are primarily oriented toward thinking are likely to develop characteristics associated with this way of arriving at conclusions: analytical inclination, objectivity, concern with principles of justice and fairness, criticality, an impassive and dispassionate demeanor, and an orientation to time that is linear, that is, concerned with connections from the past through the present and toward the future (p.13).

Finally, they describe *Feeling* as:

…the function by which one comes to decisions by weighing relative values and merits of the issues. Feeling relies on an understanding of personal values and group values; thus it is more subjective than thinking. Because values are subjective and personal, persons making judgments with the feeling function are more likely to be attuned to the values of others as well as to their own values and feelings. They try to understand people and to anticipate and take into account the effects of the decision at hand and on the people involved and on what is important to them. They have a concern with the human as opposed to the technical aspects of problems, a desire for affiliation, warmth, and harmony, a time orientation that includes preservation of enduring values (p. 14).

Putting it all together

We combine the introverted and extraverted attitudes (e and i) with the four mental functions (T,N,S,F) and get the original eight psychological types Jung created. This is presented in figure 10. As you can see each mental function has an introverted and extraverted attached to it, showing the mental function's use towards the inner world and the outer world. It helps me, in this case to think about extravert and introvert as a verb. To introvert feeling, is to focus the energy of feeling towards the self, your inner world, creating depth of feeling. To extravert feeling is to focus the energy of the feeling on to another person, object or thing, one way this can be seen is showing affection towards a person, dog, or object.

Notice that we are not done yet. The MBTI has 16 types. This only shows eight.

Figure 10

In addition to the above, Isabel Myers and Katharine Briggs decided it was wise to add another dimension pertaining to structure, structure to the outside world. Further they said it was inferred throughout Jung's writings but never specifically spelled out. They added **Judging** and **Perceiving**; **J/P**. Doubling the type count to 16 from 8. This describes our orientation to the outer world, in other words, the lifestyle favored for interacting with the outside world.

People preferring **Perceiving** are motivated by flexibility and stressed by rigid structure/schedules. For example, they are characterized by the following:

- They produce results by emerging methods that unfold in the moment or the last day or week of a deadline.

- Interruptions are viewed as a natural part of living; they live spontaneously.

- They are more reactive

- They consider other possibilities before making a decision

- The live more day-to-day, moment-to-moment

- When entering a pool, for example, they just jump into the deep end

- They are process-oriented.

People preferring **Judging** are motivated by rigid structure and schedules and stressed by flexibility. For example, they are characterized by the following:

- They produce best results by organized preparation; a sense of well-being and comfort is experienced with methodical steps and goals that need to get done in the allotted time.

- They are more proactive

- They are more closed-minded

- They prepare long-term plans

- When entering a pool, they inch in, step-by-step, gradually reaching the deep end of the pool

- They are system-oriented.

And that completes the basic understanding of typology. From this you can determine what each letter means in the type code ENTP.

To conclude this section, I will leave you with some final thoughts and some quotes. When looking for a career, a partner, or applying for a college, remember this: Knowing yourself can help you harness parts of your individuality so that you can capitalize on your strengths.

To implement this in your life, I suggest making a skill tree - mind-map. Which puts on paper your personal attributes, professional skills sets, Technical skills, career interests and preferred job titles on the right side and your weak points and areas of improvement on the left.

Watching your thoughts and actions are also important determiners in your success.

Thoughts on the four mental functions

Moving on, let's review these words from Blake W. Burleson as we consider the nature of the four mental functions

> "What should be kept in mind here is that the functions are not merely differences, they are opposites. They are as opposite as night and day, black and white. Furthermore, Jung argued that one cannot use both of these functions at same time. When one uses his head, his heart is pushed aside, and vice versa. They can be engaged alternatively, but not at the same moment." (*Pathways to Integrity*, Blake W. Burleson, p.15)

Let's consider these statistics from Myers-Briggs research and the following passage to further explain the mental functions and how it works in society.

> "The statistics from the MBTI indicate that Americans are nearly evenly divided between those who prefer thinking and those who prefer feeling, as evaluative functions. Most Americans are more familiar with the head (T) (Thinking) versus the heart (F) (Feeling) struggle of daily life" (*Pathways to Integrity*, Blake W. Burleson)

We see this in dramas and movies of all sorts. The man represses his emotions and disconnects emotionally, and the woman tries to encourage the man to speak about their "feelings". There has always been "thinking-type females" and "feeling-type males" so the opposite is true as well. This means that in the same example above, the roles could be switched; the woman represses her emotions and disconnects emotionally, and the man tries to encourage the woman speak about their "feelings".

This does not apply to sensing and intuition however:

"The data from the MBTI suggests that approximately 73.3% of Americans prefer sensing over intuition (Myers, 1998) so this playing field will not be level in American culture as the opposites compete"

Jung argued that the interplay of the opposites is essential for Psychic/mental health and well-being **("Psychic Equilibrium" as he called it.)** When one function dominates, an imbalance occurs. This imbalance can occur in a culture as well as an individual. If nearly three-fourths of Americans prefer sensing over intuition, what imbalance would one expect from a cultural perspective?

Another way to ask the question is: What are the biases of the culture?

Notice the following characteristics that develop from the sensing and intuitive functions. In doing so, consider which function is valued the most in the fields of business, education, and politics in our western culture.

In a bottom line, results-oriented, technologically-based society, the preference of institutions for the ability of (S) sensing types is apparent. (*Pathways to Integrity*, Blake W. Burleson. p. 25)

Figure 11

<table>
<tr><td>Sensing (S)</td><td>Intuition (N)</td></tr>
</table>

Sensing (S)	Intuition (N)
• *Proof*	• *Possibilities*
• *Facts*	• *Vision*
• *Result*	• *Fate*
• *Certainty*	• *Chance*
• *Know*	• *Potential*
• *Concentrate (Focus)*	• *Wonder*
• *Evident*	• *Guess/(improvise)*
• *Sensible*	• *Dream/(Day-Dream)*
• *(Detailed)*	• *Latent*
• *(Practical/Tired and True)*	• *Mindful*
	• *General (the gist of it)*

Figure 11

Because nearly 75% of people are Sensors (not Intuitives), They usually stay to the left of Figure 11, and because of this they may not see the Intuitives' visions.

Establishing Dominant Mental Functions and Inferior Mental Functions

People dominant in the intuition function grasp possibilities better, and see the potential in things; for example, a dirty, old, broken down church can be an amazing and innovative cultural center or a run-down factory can become an artist's gallery, where people come together and are unified in arts, crafts, and abilities. These people see things for what it can be not necessarily for what it is.

People dominant in sensing would see it as it is, with one of their five senses such as their eyes, not their sixth sense or "third eye." So, a dirty old church or a decrepit factory would be just what it is. They don't see the potential in it. They may just want to tear it down and make something new in its place.

Going with your natural tendencies/dominant strengths provides both efficiency and sustainability in your journey to complete your vision!

Specifically this means…

- **More focus**
- **More learning**
- **More comprehension**
- **More success**
- **More progress**

Going with your natural tendencies leads to working little and producing great results. Going against your natural tendencies leads to working too hard to produce too little. To further explain this, look at figure 12. You'll see that psychological energy is shortened to "psychic energy." It is much easier and much less strenuous to access your #1 or dominant strength and your #2, or second strongest strength, than it is to dig deep and reach for your third strongest. The most difficult of all is your fourth strongest trait.

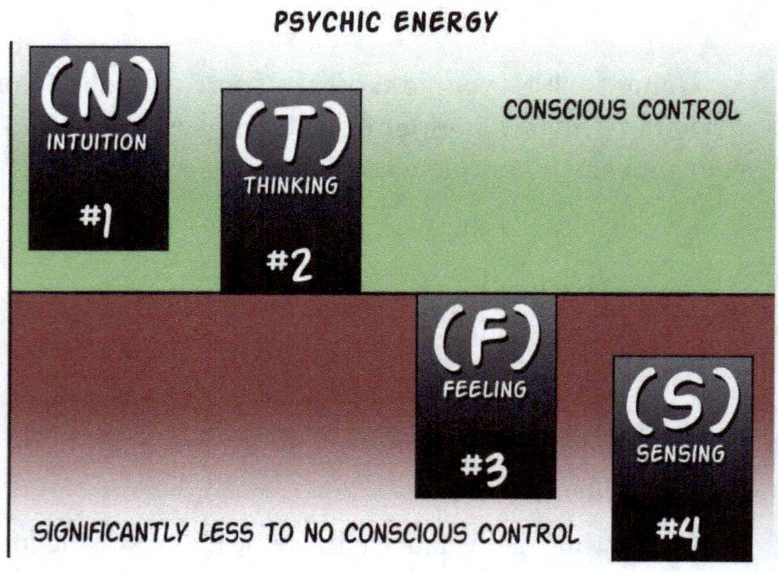

Figure 12

This illustration shows the hierarchy of consciousness among four mental functions, S, T, F, N. with #1 being your most developed strength or "Dominant Function," and #4 being your least developed and "largely unconscious" inferior function.

In the conscious control section (green) there is always one function that is evaluative and one that is information gathering. In the red section of the chart where there is less conscious control; notice that the functions are not as readily accessible as the other two. They take more mental energy.

So, for this individual, we can observe that the preferred information gathering function is *Intuition* and the evaluative function is *Thinking*. It is also showing the hierarchy of mental functions for a particular type. This graph is in direct relationship ENTP. Your type may be different than this one. So the order of the mental functions in figure 12 may differ for you, and your main strength will be different in accordance to your type.

Functions toward the top are easiest to access and take the least amount of psychological energy. Functions toward the bottom take significantly more psychological energy to access. Using your fourth strongest trait for a long period of time may result in a sense of frustration, boredom, irritation, and overall mental exhaustion.

To view this in a different way, let us consider this example, Let's say you're a "righty," that is, you prefer your right hand over your left. Your right hand would be your #1 or dominant strength, your #2 or auxiliary (second strength) would be your left hand. Your hands are more skilled then your feet; on the whole you can do more with hands then your feet. So your #3 and #4 would be your left and right foot. Imagine how frustrating and impossible it would be to try to do everything you do with your hands with your feet!

Developing Your Mental Functions

According to Jung, we are all involved in a lifelong process of striving toward completeness, becoming our best self, therefore we are always seeking to grow our mental functions. When looking to grow our mental functions it is important to notice the signs of growth.

According to the MBTI manual, these are the signs of developing mental functions:

- Conscious of the function
- Aware of its impact
- Able to control it
- Able to direct it at will
- Confident and flexible in its use

Your first or dominant function will develop and grow the strongest; therefore, it will be the one most developed and differentiated. It will have all the characteristics noted above. Your second will be strong as well, maybe missing perhaps one of the characteristics. Your third and fourth traits will not develop as clearly as the first and second; they will have fewer of the characteristics noted above and will grow less in accordance.

This philosophy of dominant to inferior functions (#1 to #4) is an extendable concept; it can be found in many personality and strength assessments. It applies to strength themes in the StrengthsFinder assessment as well.

After taking the StrengthsFinder 2.0 assessment, you will receive your top five strength themes. These are strengths that come naturally to you and are ranked from 1st to 5th in accordance to how active they are in your life. So, your first theme will be similar to your dominant function and the one you are most conscious of. Your second theme will be less active then your first, and so on.

David Kerisey's Temperament Theory and Character development

If you look up synonyms of "individuality," you will find two of special importance to Mr. Kerisey and one of special importance to Paul Tough. They are *"intelligence"* and *"temperament"* for Mr. Kerisey and *"Character"* for Mr. Tough.

I will first start with Paul Tough's comments from his book *How Children Succeed,* then go into David Kerisey.

The well-kept secret to success is "character." In his book, *How Children Succeed,* Paul Tough also lays out a list of seven character strengths that predict life satisfaction and high achievement they are:

"Grit, self-control, zest, social intelligence, gratitude, optimism and curiosity." (p.76   )

Tough continues to talk about how these character traits were incorporated into a "character report card" used in KIPP's New York City schools. Others were hesitant to adopt it but it did provide a beginning for thinking about the importance of character in developing our young students. He goes on to explain how many individuals and selected schools he studied went on to try to harvest these character traits in the children they served. Tough gives an enlightened approach to the study of how children succeed, for those interested in more detail it is a worthwhile read.

David Kerisey focuses more on intelligence and temperament than character development. According to Kerisey, There are four types of intelligence that exists within each individual, and each one is characterized by a certain temperament. This works the same way as illustrated in figure 12, in the section "Establishing Dominant Mental Functions and Inferior Mental Functions"

In David Keirsey's book *Please Understand Me II,* he describes and identifies the four types of intelligences. One is dominant and is the expression of the personality.

Below are both the hierarchy of the four intelligences and their names for the temperament of the "Idealist."

They are the…

- #1 Diplomatic (Intelligence), NF (Mental Function Pair), Idealist (Temperament)

- # 2 Strategic (Intelligence), NT (Mental Function Pair), Rational (Temperament)

- # 3 Logistical (Intelligence), SJ (Mental Function and Structure toward the Outside World), Guardian (Temperament)

- # 4 Tactical (Intelligence), SP (Mental Function and Structure toward the Outside World), Artisan (Temperament)

Notice that NF – NT are in reference to the mental function pairs we learned earlier in this chapter. Also notice the combination of a mental function and preferred structure style SJ - SP. To determine which one of the four temperaments you are, you can take the Keirsey Temperament Sorter II (KTS–II).

Knowing your temperament will provide you with significant insight in a few of life's fields, including your career education, preoccupation, and vocational interests; as well as your social roles such as mating (having a romantic relationship), parenting (with your children), and leading (your leadership style, leading any group of businessmen or women).

The difference between Psychological types and Intelligence types

It is also important to recognize David Keirsey calls the four temperaments "intelligence types." He has this to say about the difference between psychological types and intelligence types:

In considering the contrast between psychological types and intelligence types please bear in mind that Jung and Myers were trying to figure out what the different types have in mind, while I am trying to figure out what they can do well under varying circumstances.

Typology sets out to define different people's mental makeup – what's in their heads – something which is not observable, and which is thus unavoidably subjective, a matter of speculation, and occasionally of projection...

In my view, which is based on close observation of people's use of words...and 40 years or so of type watching...I base my type definitions on what people do well, their skilled actions what I called their 'intelligent roles' which are observable and thus can be defined more objectively (David Keirsey, *Please Understand Me II*, pgs. 30, 341)

Also, notice the words he's using for temperament; Keirsey says they originate from Plato, Plato was a philosopher and mathematician in Classical Greece, around c340 BC. The words used are *idealist, rational, artisan,* and *guardian.* As time went on this temperament theory fell into the lap of Roman physician Claudius Galen and it was he who fleshed out the theory around 190 A.D. in his book the *Theory of Humors.*

In *Theory of Humors* there are four types, I have matched them up with the four temperaments: sanguine *(artisan),* choleric *(idealist),* phlegmatic *(rational),* and melancholic *(guardian).*

In *Please Understand Me II*, Keirsey quotes Galen's work:

> That it is neither the stars nor the gods that
> determine what we want and what we do; rather,
> it is the balance of our bodily fluids the four
> 'humors' as they were called… Thus for the first
> time, in the West at any rate, our physiology was
> said to determine our attitudes and actions, and
> not the deities or heavenly bodies….(p. 23)

Kiersey continues:

….So the idea that individuals are predisposed to develop into one of four different configurations of attitude and action has survived for well over 2000 years. Surely this idea (of types) would not have been employed for so long, by so many people, in so many countries, had there not been some sort of widely shared recognition of its usefulness…

…That the characteristics of the four temperaments are this consistent over time is no accident, but seems to reflect a fundamental pattern...of human nature. (*Please Understand Me II*, Keirsey (p. 23–26).

Kathy Kolbe adds her contribution

As time passed Kathy Kolbe got her hands on these personality theories, she read it all from Jung to Myers to Keirsey. She noticed that all the current theories have something to do with your emotional or cognitive attitude. No one was talking about the "Conative connection"

What Kathy Kolbe saw differently is best described by explaining the three parts of the mind. Most personality assessments focus on the cognitive and affective parts of the mind. Kolbe focuses on the Conative, seen in the three parts of mind explained below:

1. **Cognitive (Thinking)** – Thoughts, intelligence, learned behaviors, knowledge, recall, skills.

2. **Conative (Doing)** – Purposeful action, drives, urges, natural abilities, innate talents, MO, instincts.

3. **Affective (Feeling)** – Feelings, emotions, personality, preferences, desires, attitudes, values. (*Powered by Instinct,* Kathy Kolbe, p. 17).

Conative is part of the "doing" section of the mind, and it drives your MO. Kathy Kolbe's assessments evaluate your MO and your unique way of striving and taking action.

In essence, what you think about and the way you feel about something drives the actions that you take. The mid-point here is where your thinking and feeling come together at one point to make the conative.

Kathy Kolbe explains her four action modes:

"Fact Finder - The instinctive need to gather information.

Follow Thru - The instinctive need to organize, store and retrieve information.

Quick Start - The instinctive need to deal with (risk) and unknowns.

Implementer - The instinctive need to deal with space and physical elements (tangibles)." (Kathy Kolbe, *Powered by Instinct*, p. 61).

Then Kolbe gives you your arrangement of these four action modes on a scale from 1 to 10. So your arrangement could be 8-4-3-2, which means; 8 for fact finder, 4 for follow thru, 3 for quick start, 2 for implementer.

Just as the psychic energy chart shows (figure 12) you will have a dominant (#1) MO (Modus Operdi), which will use the most instinctive energy and three other MOs that are in varying degrees different than the second, third, and fourth.

Kathy Kolbe also leaves us with this parting wisdom by sharing a dialogue she had with a client:

Kathy: You don't always get to do what you *want* to do. But you won't accomplish anything if you don't ignite your own instincts. Don't wait to respond to others. Create your own opportunities. Then you can fight for the freedom to do what you do in your own way.

Eve: Why should I have to *fight* for that? Aren't I *entitled* to be free to be me?

Kathy: **Having the right to personal liberty—which I believe includes acting according to our instincts— doesn't ensure that the freedom will always be there.** Just as our nation has to do battle to keep our liberty a reality, **so you have to take action to ensure that you're free to be your authentic self.** (*Powered by Instinct,* Kathy Kolbe, p. 50). (Emphasis added in bold)

Joseph Campbell also seems to be aligned with the above quote. On the back cover of *Reflections on the Art of Living,* he says

"The privilege of a lifetime is being who you are."

Now that you have read both Chapter five and Chapter six.

It's time to take out a journal and write out what helped you most .

In chapter five, What are some of the skills you specialize in

What makes you unique?

In Chapter six,

Have you taken the Myers Briggs ? What's your type?
Have you taken the Kolbe? What's your four numbers?
Have you taken the Strength Finders Assessment ? What's your top five themes.

Applications for personality type

The goal in understanding all these personality theories and theories on individuality is to find who you are and how we can come together in a group. No man is an island. We are our strongest when we unite!

As Carl Jung once said, **"If a plant is to unfold its specific nature to the full, it must first be able to grow in the soil in which it is planted."** (*Psychological Types* by C. G. Jung)

Like a plant adapting to its soil, it is important to seek self-improvement and grow into the person you were meant to be.

You need to establish yourself as an individual who has certain strengths and core competencies. Establishing this individuality allows you to be a more productive and a more effective member of society. Once you know your unique contribution to the group, using you individual strengths, you can be an effective team player.

We each have an important contribution to society, but it is our job to find ourselves and then place ourselves in the area that aligns with who we are. This is valuable because now you will know where you fit in. You will *do what you are!*

Like pieces of a complex puzzle, we are *independently interdependent*. This concept works well with the business world in mind. In a successful business, each department contributes to the integrity of the whole. All departments are independent and interdependent; they are all part of the same organization working toward the same goals in unity; whether they are in on building or not.

In the literature we find this concept as well. Let's consider the following quote from the Scriptures:

> "For just as each of us has one body with many members, and these members do not all have the same function, so in Christ we, though many, form one body, and each member belongs to all the others. We have different gifts, according to the grace given to each of us…"

The Holy Bible (Romans 12:4-6, NIV)

Working with clients: A case study

Charles is an individual with many talents and dreams. He did not know how to cultivate these talents and how to best pursue his dreams and become the hero in his own journey. The following case study is of a client named Charles who finally made the move to a better job through the coaching process.

My client is a single parent, his son lives with him. Living in his ordinary world, things are going okay, but he's living paycheck to paycheck with his janitorial job. He heard the call to adventure a couple of times and worked temporarily at his dream job, working at a radio station with Howard Stern. However, after a while Charles retreated back to his janitor job where he was paid a steady income. It was comfortable for him it paid the bills. Until one day, he was fed up and he called on a coach (like me) to bring him back to the job he always dreamed about. He was committed to the task. We worked together to help him achieve his vision. We took a look at the traditional radio stations, XM radio and Sirius Satellite radio. We worked on his resume, capitalizing on his strengths which were found out from his Myers Briggs results.

He also took the *Keirsey Temperament Sorter* and was able to highlight his strengths when going on the interview and finally he took the Kolbe Assessment and found out his unique way of taking action, so when the negotiations for salary started, we knew how to position him as an expert. This, along with some role-playing and encouragement, gave Charles the determination he needed.

He was ready to find his place in the radio world. He went to networking groups and career fairs specifically catered to people interested in being on the radio. He met with some resistance and got some no's but also found some people that were in the same situation he was in. They formed an alliance and started working together, soon enough they met with people that where "in the know" and they introduced him to positions that were not posted on job boards and websites.

This was his shot. Charles spent money on a nice new suit.With some encouragement, the solid understanding of himself and his value to a prospective employer, he was ready. He waited anxiously to meet the hiring manager of XM radio. He spoke about his previous experience and strengths, and then he made a joke. They were having a great time, laughing and joking. Charles thought it was a good time to pitch his idea for the next radio show; it was going to be something along the lines of the *Abbott and Costello Show*. The hiring manager liked his idea for the new radio show and after reviewing a couple candidates, the hiring manager picked Charles. Charles was confident in his abilities and it showed.

Naturally there was a celebration, but the real test was his first week on the job. Charles had to really nail it and bring the ratings way up, to show the hiring manager he was the right one for the job. His anxiety got the best of him in his third show, but he was able to center himself and rely on his instincts to bring him through successfully. He has now been working there for a couple months and gets paid more than he did at his previous janitor job and he's a lot happier too!

This is just one example of how things can work out for you when you apply yourself and seek counsel for your vision.

Individual Leadership

You exercise individual leadership by getting these personality assessments administered, interpreted and applied to your situation. You will get better insight on your leadership style and how you function; it should be used as a mirror to reflect the positive and negative aspects of your personality in order to reach your full potential.

Below are some examples. These are preferred methods of gathering and processing information according to type.

When **gathering information for what you don't know,** every person has a particular preference or way of proceeding,

Some do it best from sight, watching an expert.

Others do it best by hearing.

Others do it best through touch.

Still others learn best from engaging their sixth sense (engaging their imagination)

When **processing information** to perform their best:

Some need to get their whole body involved in some kind of movement such as dance or running.

Some need to use their hands or play with something in their hands.

Others need to talk it out with speech; intellectualize it.

Still others need to picture it with their imagination.

This is loosely based on Walter Lowen's book *Dichotomies of Mind*. It was originally sourced in the Type Reporter, an article named *Type and the Brain*.

Type and communication styles of individual leadership

Intuitive types are going to be okay with a very loose common ground with few clarifying questions; using descriptive language will stir the imagination.

Feeling types can pick up on emotions very quickly and accurately; they want to know if their idea is being respected first and foremost. Thereafter, feeling types will want to know that you are as excited as they are. Emotion is how their train of thought runs, so shutting them down before they are getting excited or not giving them enough fuel for their engines is just disruptive.

Sensing types will want to hear you speak about facts, practical, easy-to-connect pieces, making obvious conclusions. They can be more technical, and your clarifying questions will arise when they start using jargon or industry specific words.

Finally, thinking types will like to see the cause and effect relationships. They are logical, linear, enjoy a calm tone, and are more fluid in their thinking. These types are also more decisive.

Team Leadership and good teamwork are another great application of knowing personality type and its theory.

Given that each personality has certain strengths over others. Pairing people up in a team that has complementary strengths will lead to better decision making. You can even gather certain teams of people around a goal that you have for maximum efficiency.

To assist you in understanding teamwork, consider the following mind map on teamwork, figure 13

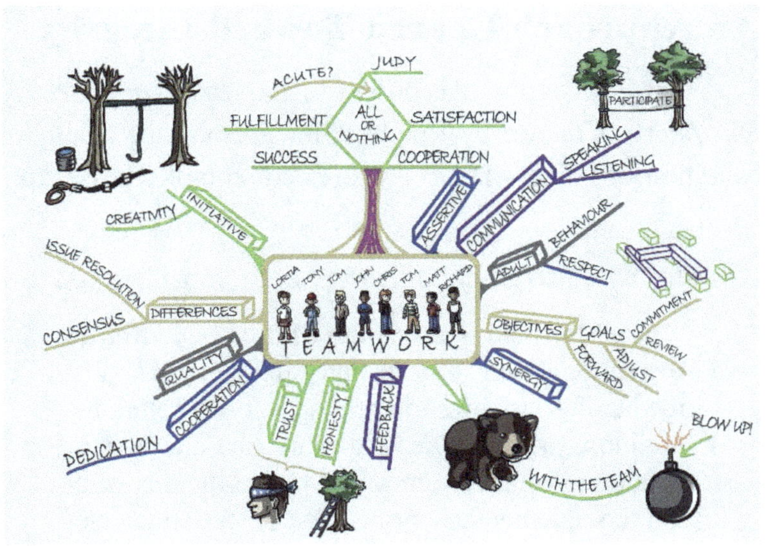

Figure 13

Ultimately, the goal in understanding all these personality theories and theories on individuality is to find who you are and how we can come together in a group. No man is an island. We are our strongest when we unite!

However, it seems that we forgotten this. In today's society, so many people are looking to be independent, do it themselves, and be separate. But as the hero's journey suggests the only reason you separate is to alleviate a problem or issue that exists. Once the solution is made it is of upmost importance then to complete the journey and re-integrate, return back to society.

In essence, what I am speaking about is integrity, not so much in the sense of a moral code, but in being whole.

An Approach Geared Toward Integrity

What is integrity? According to the *American Heritage Dictionary* as quoted by Burelson, integrity is "the quality or condition of being whole or undivided; completeness." (pg. 93)

What could represent integrity? Let's consider this:

> **A Mandala is a symbol of oneness, totality or integration**. Typically, it is used for meditative visualization among various religious traditions while expressing unity, the alternating quadrants within are meant to depict the dualistic but complementary principles of the universe (*Pathways to Integrity*, Blake W. Burleson, p. 60).

In light of this, I have created my own mandala using the mental functions as guides. In the upcoming pages, I present a whole-brain mandala. The image has many uses. **The first** is to use and explain whole-brain thinking as a way towards holistic/moral decision making; **the second** is to show the mental functions in different pairs; and **the third** is to show how people are different because of their preferred mental function pairs.

Let's start with the first purpose. Look at the center of the image, (figure 14). Notice the trucks that have brought the mental functions down the road. They have dumped the functions into the center pot emitting steam. This imagery aims to portray the process of whole-brain thinking; which has holistic/moral decision-making as its goal. Once each function and the information it offers has been recognized, understood, and dumped into the center pot, the steam can start to be produced. Notice that the mental functions are all together in one center pot—expressing unity.

The steam symbolizes the synthesis of the four mental functions achieving whole-brain thinking. Whole-brain thinking is a technique that one uses both of your brain's hemispheres. This, of course, is in an effort to balance your approach toward problems and challenges, giving you the widest awareness of the whole. The idea here is that after you can see the issues and problems you face in a holistic or whole sense, solutions will always emerge.

Problems contain the seeds of their own solutions; you just need to flesh out the problems to find the solutions. The whole brain mandala gives you a framework for fleshing out problems.

Start at sensing (S) what you know about the problem, obvious details and things that can be easily observed with the senses. Then go to intuition (N). Look into any hidden meanings, patterns, connectors, or relationships; Then use thinking (T) by looking objectively at the problems, using cause-and-effect to link ideas together to make logical connections. Finally use feeling (F) by weighing relative values and the merits of the issues. Understand personal values and group values. Put yourself in the other person's shoes with a concern for their well-being and harmony.

The second use of the whole brain mandala is to show the different arrangements of mental functions. We have **mental function pairs**, otherwise known as the "cognitive core" of the personality as described previously. They are diagonal to one another, the (ST)–(NF) and (SF)–(NT), and they are opposites. Because they are opposites, they have the potential for conflict. However, if the individuals could put away their differences and check their situations, problems, or arguments with one another in a constructive sense, their stance could not only be challenged but more importantly significantly strengthened. In essence, the person delegates his or her weakness or inferior function to someone that has that weakness as strength. Their joined effort will lead to more production and more achievement. You can also look at it as two sides of the brain (as in the left and right hemispheres).

The third use of the whole-brain mandala is to show how people are different because of their preferred mental function pairs. The mental function pair is, in essence, the cognitive core of the personality and the dominant way of looking at the world. When you look at the mandala, you can see these mental function pairs as the four quadrants.

In *Pathways to Integrity*, Burleson explains that:

> Jung argued that such wholeness, while rare, is the task of all human beings. In moral decision-making, the use of all four psychological functions enables us to be the reliable captain of our own ship as well encounter new frontiers. (B. W. Burleson, p. 29–30).

As you will see in this mandala, (Figure 14), the left and the right hemispheres are labeled (S) sensing and (N) intuition with (S) being the left side of the brain and (N) being the right side of the brain.

The Whole Brain Mandala

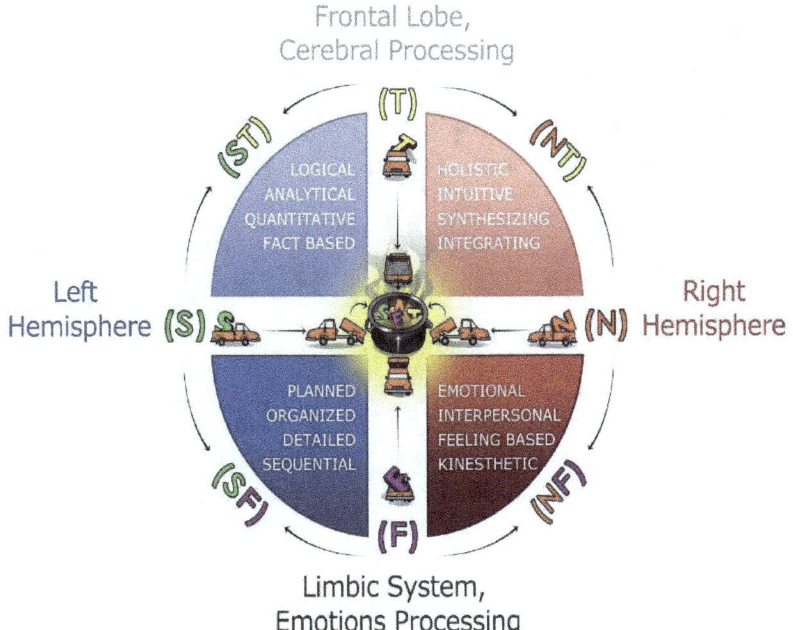

Figure 14

With guidance and your willingness to see other perspectives you will enhance your decision making process. In this sense, you can make the entire four quadrants one, and achieve "wholeness."

The ultimate goal, albeit an ideal one, is full engagement in your body (S), heart (F), mind (T), and intuition (N). Reconciling all of this information helps you to eradicate illusions and crystalize your decision-making. Seeing things clearly gives you the confidence to overcome rejection and objection from any outside force.

The easiest way to activate this "whole-brain thinking" is to become more engaged in your activity. We will be speaking about this in the next chapter.

This process of whole brain thinking will come clearer in the next chapter. As you will see, it comes more natural when you are at the higher levels of engagement.

C H A P T E R 8

Building Mental and Emotional Engagement

If you want to increase production, you need to be more engaged. When you are more engaged, you can use anabolic energy as the source from which you draw instead of catabolic energy.

At this point, the hero is at the central ordeal. Towards the end of the chapter you will see what happens when he encounters the dragon, you will learn about the reward as well. At this time, the hero just needs to stay engaged and see the vision through to the end. In terms of the hero's journey this chapter covers step 8 and step 9.

In this chapter, we will explore concepts revolving around the idea of engagement. We will start with catabolic and anabolic energy, then go into talking about the stress evaluator, energy blocks, challenges on your path to success, and how to overcome them with your own effort and the *Inner Wisdom Internet.*

Catabolic and Anabolic Energy

There are two sources of energy, catabolic and anabolic. These are the sources of energy that one can be using to keep others engaged during work. Below is an example of their leadership styles.

Bruce Schneider, president of the Institute for Professional Excellence in Coaching (IPEC) points out the difference between *anabolic* and *catabolic* leaders in his book:

Are You a Catabolic or Anabolic Leader?

The Catabolic Leader	*The Anabolic Leader*
• Manages: Controls by pushing and pulling	• Leads: Encourages others to take their own steps
• Delegates fully (and then points and blames)	• Project shares (becomes part of the plan)
• Gives information without justification or buy-in	• Shares (detailed) information and gets feedback and buy-in
• Self assesses	• Utilizes others' feedback
• Works in crisis mode	• Plans and develops, is future focused
• Emotionally disconnects	• Utilizes emotional intelligence
• Uses left brain analysis	• Uses whole brain thinking
• Focuses on problems	• Sees only opportunities
• Takes advantage of staff	• Sees the true human resource

Ideal leaders are anabolic leaders. They create and attract success. Anabolic leaders have the ability to motivate and inspire themselves and others to do extraordinary things. They have the ability to make energetic shifts in all levels of the organization

Employees are positive and productive when they feel confident about their leader. They want to believe that their leader is strong, resilient, insightful, and able to take care of both the company and their personal needs.

When a leader resonates with catabolic energy, chaos often ensues. Employees no longer feel they're walking on a firm foundation. They tread cautiously to make sure they don't fall.

A catabolic leader is not the result of the challenge. A catabolic leader *is* the challenge. Catabolic leaders break down nearly all aspects of the company, including the people in it. You may be shocked to learn that nearly 85% of all leaders are actually catabolic; they destroy the energy and momentum of the people around them as well as their companies and families as a whole.

(*Energy Leadership*, Bruce Schneider, pgs. 79, 81).

The person with catabolic energy maintains a constant awareness of just the problem, and they fail to provide solutions. Although the person may seem highly engaged in getting what they want, their catabolic energy is limiting their enthusiasm. Their collaboration could be deemed disruptive, and therefore, doesn't allow a flow. They do not allow an effortless flow of ideas in the direction of their dreams as would someone with an anabolic output.

Anabolic leaders use "whole-brain thinking" (explained in Chapter 7). It goes by many names; "holographic" thinking, holistic decision making, and moral decision making. Using this technique leads to the utmost integrity!

Consider leaders during the Medieval times between the Dark Ages and the Middle Ages. Anabolic leaders were like the benevolent kings, the brave hearts that instilled loyalty, unity, and compassion. Catabolic leaders were the tyrannical kings, belittling their supporters and instilling fear.

In this sense, success in a project is about taking out the catabolic people that are not working with the team and are thus being disruptive.

Lastly, understanding anabolic and catabolic energy on a more bodily level is very interesting consider this situation:

> When the mind perceives a threat, anabolic hormones, such as testosterone, decreases, while the catabolic hormones, such as cortisol, adrenalin, increase. The increase in catabolic hormones serves a short-term purpose by creating enough physical energy to meet the stressor.
>
> However, on a long-term basis, a constant release of catabolic hormones deteriorates the entire physical system.
>
> Both types of hormonal releases stem from thoughts; therefore, thoughts are either anabolic or catabolic. Each of us has trained ourselves to automatically react to many of our life situations. These 'default tendencies' if catabolic, actually cannibalize our entire system. *(Energy Leadership*, Bruce Schneider, p. 13)

There are seven levels of engagement, and each level corresponds to a greater number of production.

In figure 16, the lower levels (1-2) relate to lower levels of production and catabolic energy. The higher levels (3-7) relate to higher levels of production and anabolic energy. Anabolic energy is constructive, solution-oriented; catabolic energy typically is destructive and problem-oriented. Both are needed to a certain extent. With no awareness of a problem, there is no solution to be found. See chart below.

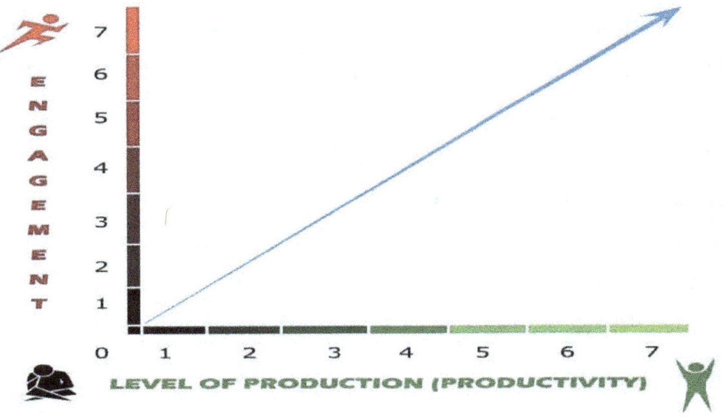

As noted, lower levels of engagement and production (1-2) are associated with catabolic energy. Catabolic energy, if sustained and used over a long time, leads to the same results as Quadrant I in Stephan Covey's *Seven Habits of Highly Effective People*, Time Management Matrix, (p. 152)

I reference Stephan Covey's work here because it is a valuable source for those that are looking for a more specific way to categorize types of behavior. More information about his four quadrant system can be found in this book. For now, I reference two quadrants: 1 and 2, these quadrants speak about the two types of energy we have been discussing.

The results of spending time in Quadrant I are:

1. Burn-out
2. Stress
3. Always Putting out fires (running from one emergency to the next one, not getting real productive work done)
4. Time spent on problems and crisis management

The activities in this quadrant are urgent and important. Unfortunately, Quadrant I consumes many. Overall, individuals in this stage have low energy and enthusiasm for the work. At engagement level one, the core thought is, "I'm a victim," and the core feeling is apathy, which leaves them lethargic and not wanting to do anything. They may be asking themselves questions such as, "Why does this always happen to me?" "Why do I have to always put out these fires?" "Why am I always working in crisis-mode running to the next pressing problem?"

The higher levels (3-7) are related to higher levels of production and anabolic energy. If sustained and used over a long time, this leads to the same results as Quadrant II as presented in Stephan Covey's *Seven Habits of Highly Effective People*, Time Management Matrix, (p. 154).

The results of spending time in Quadrant II are:

1. **Vision**

2. Perspective

3. Balance

Although important, the activities that one participates in this quadrant (such as relationship-building or recognizing new opportunities) are **not urgent**. Because they're not urgent, people tend to forget about them. In Stephan Covey's research which focuses on a group of shopping center managers, this is what he found:

> We did an analysis of the time they (shopping center managers) were spending on that activity (Quadrant II activity, such as relationship building or recognizing new opportunities). It was less than 5 percent. They had good reasons—problems, one right after another. They had reports to make out, meetings to go to, correspondence to answer, phone calls to make, constant interruptions. Quadrant I had consumed them. (Seven Habits of Highly Effective People, Stephan Covey, p. 155)

In Covey's Time Management Matrix, quadrants 3 and 4 have to do unimportant tasks such as interruptions and time wasters.

At engagement levels 5, 6, and 7, you gain access to more powerful techniques and abilities such as **recognition of win,**

win opportunities, and **synthesis** (being able to synthesize large pieces of information).

Creation is essentially creatively looking at the problem from different perspectives and accessing "whole-brain thinking" (explained in Chapter 7).

Doing more than one thing

The problem in our current society is we are so busy doing, doing, and more doing that we forget about being. What does being mean? It means really being, living in the moment, and experiencing what it means to be a human being, not a human doing.

This challenge has affected us in the form of effort, time, and attention. Short attention spans are popping up everywhere; this has the consequence of reduced focus on just one thing. The increase in this kind of behavior is largely due to the way we get information. To some, it feels as if we are getting bombarded by multiple sources of media, and each one is competing for our attention, pulling us in different directions. As a result, we are seeing more and more people involved in more than just one activity. For some, our minds and bodies are going in five different directions. This is not productive! When we are pulled in so many directions, it can take us away from our "central goal". The time it takes to refocus on that one thing you are trying to accomplish can take a long time.

When you are concerned with just *one* activity and everything it has to offer, your outcomes are more accurate, precise, and detailed. The key is to think big picture—what is the one thing you can do that will have the most impact on your goals? Furthermore, it is important to focus on the present, what needs to be accomplished now, not the past or mistakes you made. There is a saying: Yesterday is history, tomorrow is a mystery, but today is a gift. That's why they call it the present!

Strictly speaking, this philosophy of engagement is a way of life. It speaks of putting 100% of your effort and energy into whatever you do. It is perhaps best described in a section called "No Trace" from *Zen Mind, Beginner's Mind* by Shunryu Suzuki: "When you do something, you should burn yourself completely, like a good bonfire [which leaves only white ash] leaving no trace of yourself [behind]." (p. 64). Suzuki continues later in the section saying:

> To leave a trace is not the same as to remember something. It is necessary to remember what we have done, but we should not become attached to what we have done in some special sense. What we call 'attachment' is just these traces of our thought and activity.

> In order not to leave any traces, when you do something, you should do it with your whole body and mind; you should be concentrated on what you do. You should do it completely, like a good bonfire. (*Zen Mind, Beginner's Mind,* p. 66)

Give it your all! The activity transforms you and when you are finished, you jump out into a new transformed self, dying to the previous self, in the process. You are re-born. Probably the most relatable real-world example of this is going to the gym with intense aggravation and frustration. But when you are finished you are different. The aggravation and frustration has been alleviated. You have, in a sense, "burned it off" leaving "no trace" at the gym.

Finding your optimal level of engagement is related to the right amount of stress. Finding the right amount of stress is dependent on your self-understanding. This is not easy, however like anything else in life being successful at it takes constant effort, and it is important not to get too excited about the result and breeze through the process. This is especially true with regard to understanding yourself.

Shunryu Suzuki has the following to say about building character:

> Building character is like making bread – you have to mix it little by little, step by step, and moderate temperature is needed. You know yourself quite well, and you know how much temperature you need. You know exactly what you need. But if you get too excited, you will forget how much temperature is good for you, and you will lose your own way. This is very dangerous. *(Zen Mind, Beginner's Mind,* Shunryu Suzuki, p. 57)

When Suzuki says, "moderate temperature is needed," the key to this passage is revealed: How much is too much temperature? You need to know that and be aware of it. A real judge of character is not what you do when everything is in your favor, but rather when it is not, and you are under pressure and stressed. It is revealed not in times of joy but during times of crisis.

When Suzuki says that "you know how much temperature you need," this is in reference to a sports psychology idea, which states that each player must know his or her certain level of stress to be a productive player in the game. In basketball for example, if you are too relaxed, you will miss shots; if you are too excited, then you are emotionally hijacked and cannot focus properly.

You may be asking yourself, how does one increase temperature when one is too relaxed? To increase temperature

you must be able to provoke yourself into action. To further explain this concept, Kathy Kolbe, offers these words:

> You often have to goad yourself to initiate the action you desire. Let's say you're tired, listless, and have trouble getting up and going in the morning. If you don't give in to that, and instead you provoke yourself into action, you'll be off and running (Kathy Kolbe, *Powered by Instinct*, p. 49).

When you use this technique of "**self-provoking**" you enable self-motivation, which leads to:

- Inspiring your own achievements

- Directing your energies

- Pushing yourself into action

- Making what you want to happen, happen

- Igniting your own instincts

- Creating your own opportunities

(Kathy Kolbe, *Powered by Instinct*, p. 49).

It's also quite possible you're tired, listless, and have trouble getting up in the morning because you're going against your instincts.

Just like going against the grain causes friction and

struggle, going against your natural tendencies causes incongruities in your life. This leaves you mentally exhausted!

Finding the middle ground where you perform the best can be difficult. To help you, I have provided an illustration below called "The Stress Evaluator,"

Traditionally, the response to stress has been known as "fight or flight." In the illustration that follows, I propose that there is a zone of performance between the flight stage and the fight stage where we are channeling our energy to be "in the flow." This is where we have our best performance.

The zone of performance is an individual preference. Some need be closer to the 3-4 with less stress/pressure/temperature than others; some need to be closer to the 6-7 with more stress/pressure/temperature to reach the point where they are being productive.

Finding your peak zone of performance

The Stress Evaluator

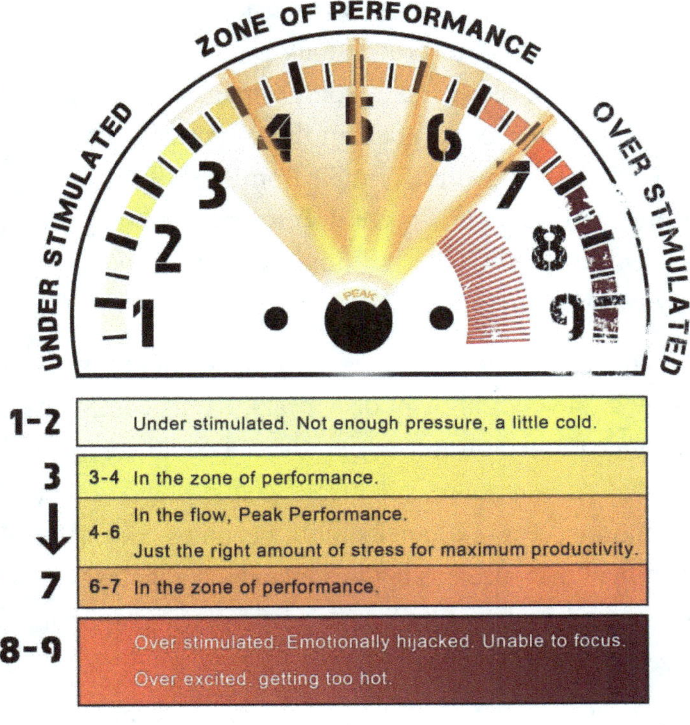

Figure
15

Your optimal level of performance is also described by Mihaly Csikszentmihalyi in his book *Flow: The Psychology of Optimal Experience*. In the book, he describes being fully engaged as the state of flow, defined as a state of concentration or complete absorption with the activity and the situation at hand. This means being both mentally and

emotionally engaged; they are united, and when united, they produce the feeling of the optimal experience.

Engagement in the Workplace

We have taken some time to talk about engagement and how it is related to production / productivity for the individual. Now let's take some time to see how engagement is related to goals in the workplace. This is done with the following formula from Stephen Kraus' **Commitment to Goal = Goal Importance (why do you want it?) × Goal Attainability** (*Psychological Foundations of Success*, p. 79).

If either goal importance or goal attainability is eliminated, the commitment disappears. Kraus continues to elaborate on his formula saying that: "People are most committed to important, attainable goals, but if either goal importance or goal attainability becomes zero, then commitment disappears. This formula also indicates why employees are often reluctant to commit to corporate goals set by senior management" (p. 80).

To further explain the ideas of goal attainability and goal importance, imagine you're a Sales Associate for a company in Corporate America. In fact, you're the #1 Sales Associate based on the three most important metrics and taking into account six states from the east coast of the US. This includes 30 teams of 10 people. Your personal best is 20 sales in a month. If they set the quota at 30 sales a month, and the number one salesman has only hit 20, this makes the goal seem unattainable. Fostering this sense of unattainability other employees think if the #1 guy can't do it, what makes management think the rest of us can do it!?

In fact, Stephen Kraus explains that in some companies: "…corporate management itself considers the goals unattainable, and merely set them outrageously high in a manipulative attempt to spur productivity" (p. 80).

Obviously, this doesn't work—it reduces productivity and commitment.

What does work is when companies support their employees by fostering a sense of attainability via training programs, hiring additional staff to share the work load, keeping them more motivated and accountable, and investing in technology to make the sales go more quickly and efficiently. Companies can also communicate why meeting and exceeding the standard sales quota is important to the employee via incentives or career growth. For example, if the salesman were to hit 20 sales, they would earn double commission straight back to the first sale. Another incentive could be a week's paid vacation. The employer could even suggest career growth. Keep in mind career growth can be tricky; it shouldn't be a manipulative attempt to spur productivity.

To further explain this tricky situation, let's explore an industrial/organizational psychology concept called **Expectancy Theory.** It assesses "valence," which is similar to goal importance. It's the value of an outcome or reward to a person. It's the extent to which one wants or desires something. In the job setting, money is a common reward that can have different valence levels for different people.

It also looks at "instrumentality," which states that a valued or important goal is going will be reached if you complete the steps and processes needed to attain it. In short, if your goal is to lose weight, and you do X amount of work you will lose X amount of pounds. Here, the valued outcome is obviously losing weight, but let's go back to the career growth idea and take something that most people consider a valued or important goal: a promotion. You come into work, and you work hard, very hard. You behave like you already occupy the position and show that you have the behaviors, skills, results and competence needed to get the job done at a satisfactory level. These behaviors show you are capable of getting the promotion. But, this promotion is two-fold—on the one hand is the employee's side, and on the other hand is the employer's side.

On the employee's side, you possess the qualities and behaviors necessary to get the promotion. On the employer's side, he has to be honest. The position must actually be open, meaning the company *is currently* seeking to fill the position.

Now, the question of trust comes in. If your boss gives you a speech about your promotion, is it just talk or is it true? Will upper management follow it? Do you believe him?

If everyone agrees—the managers, the CEO, and all persons responsible, and there is a common ground of communication and understanding at your place of business on this verbal plan, then, yes. Most would and should believe the promotion could be attained. It's reassuring, and it gives you a lot of motivation to know that if you go through every measure and do exactly what the boss asks, you will received what is promised.

But what if this backfires? You did all the steps necessary, you did better than your peers, you were told you'd receive the promotion as promised, but they did not offer it to you. Instead, they favored nepotism—the friends and family plan. They let you down. You trusted that they would honor the verbal plan and offer you the promotion, but they didn't.

They give the promotion to Jimmy across the hall, clearly inferior to your skills, knowledge, and production on all the important metrics. Because Jimmy is the manager's brother, however, they picked him. To justify their choice, they used a metric that doesn't hold the same weight as others do. Naturally, anger and frustration set in. An assumption is created that day—the assumption is that "hard work doesn't pay off." This assumption is now holding you back from working hard again, because of self-preservation, you don't want to be upset and hurt again. You simply do not take your job seriously anymore. Assumptions, like this one, are called energy blocks.

So what went wrong? Well, one solution that can be made here to increase commitment and engagement is to demand a written plan. This way its keeps both the employer and employee honest. Now you have contractual obligation, perhaps even a checklist of things you need to do, such as beat the quota for 6 months in a row, recruit 5 people, and personally train them to reach or exceed the quota for 3 months. Writing all of this down prevents any kind of upset from happening in the first place.

Assumptions come in many forms; here is another one:

Let's say you have a less-than-stellar track record. You might hear: "Oh well, how can I believe you? You don't have a good track record." If someone says this to you, you'll have no motivation to succeed. What this is doing is creating a level of uncertainty. Belief drops, doubt sets in, and you say things such as, "What am I fighting for?" There is no candle of hope to light up this darkness. This is a serious energy block.

These assumptions are examples of one of the four inner energy blocks according to the Institute for Professional Excellence in Coaching (IPEC). The other three are overcoming limiting beliefs, wrong interpretations, and the inner critic. Breaking through these energy blocks are what coaches do best. The worst of these is the inner critic.

What Can Stop You

It's common knowledge that one of the great indicators of success is attitude. Common wisdom says, "Your attitude determines your latitude," and "the sky's the limit." In fact, the only ceiling or cap put on your success is the one that you put on yourself.

In his book *Change Your Brain, Change Your Life*, Dr. Daniel G. Amen offers some uncommon knowledge on energy blocks. One of the main things he advocates is to eliminate "ANTs" (Automatic Negative Thoughts).

Here is a summary that Dr. Amen offers of some familiar **ANTs** that the **"inner critic"** likes to use:

- **Always/never thinking** — thinking in words like *always, never, no one, everyone, every time, everything.*

- **Focusing on the Negative** — seeing only the bad in the situation.

- **Fortune Felling** — predicting the worst possible outcome to a situation.

- **Mind Reading**— believing that you know what others are thinking, even though they haven't told you.

- **Thinking with Your Feelings**— believing negative feelings without ever questioning them.

- **Guilt Beating**— thinking in words like *should, must, ought,* or *have to.*

- **Labeling**— attaching a negative label to yourself or to someone else.

- **Personalizing**— investing innocuous events with personal meaning.

- **Blaming**— blaming someone else for your own problems.

(*Change Your Brain, Change Your Life*, Daniel G. Amen, p. 64)

We talk ourselves into doing things all the time; most of the time its negative self-talk, and that's when these "**ANTs**" kick in.

But what if we could stop these automatic negative thoughts and use self-talk to get something positive done? For example, How could you look at a situation like complaining in a different way, see it as an opportunity instead of a problem?

You could say that in complaining you are processing the issue, and the more you process the issue, the more you understand it, the closer you get to a solution.

The Story of the Dragon

Let's talk about the story of the dragon to point out another thing that might stop you. A dragon stands in your way. Similar to a guardian, it blocks you from achieving your greatest potential, waiting at the beginning of every new adventure. The dragon represents fear. The fight between the hero (you) and dragon starts the moment you take a step forward, and this is where a chase starts. It continues until the attainment and victory of the goal or desire is reached. In this battle, it's about who will give up first. Will the dragon hold you back, or will you continue forward, towards your goal?

When you use your will, constant perseverance, and determination to bring your inner desires to fruition, you start to establish an internal locus of control, meaning you start to understand that the factors leading up to the successes that you desire are controllable based on your own efforts. Feeling that you have a grasp over external factors gives you strong conviction in the hope you can accomplish anything you put your mind to. To the contrary, you can just sit around and do nothing about your desires, ambitions, and dreams. The external affects the internal, which in turn affects your belief in yourself and thereby preventing you from succeeding. You start to tell yourself excuses as to why you can't do something usually because of some external circumstances out of your control. Now, because you take no action on your desires, ambitions, and dreams they just add up and weigh you down. This situation, in effect, takes action on <u>you</u>. It is easier to fail if you let the external circumstances of your life control you, because it's making you think things are out of your control. It is more difficult to fail if you have the internal determination and the resolve to win, because this will always push you toward solutions and victory. This will, of course, affect your level of success. Simply put, if you are letting your external surroundings defeat you, the dragon is winning.

Following the idea of internal focus of control means that you are taking charge of your life. No more "playing the victim." This may open you to criticism and feel vulnerable but that is the chance you need to be prepared to take, a danger you need to be prepared to face. So, let's cut to the chase. Having this kind of attitude, your resolve becomes strong, and you do not allow external factors to bring you down. This way, you continue to move forward in progress of the goal. You have the power to change your destiny! You have the strength to overcome your external dragons.

Joseph Campbell describes this **dragon** as having scales that have something written on them. They all say, "Thou shall not…," referring to your limited beliefs, past assumptions, past interpretations, and your previously mentioned inner critic. These fears and energy blocks were put there by you to protect you—it's sort of a self-preservation you created.

Figure 18

The Dragon Guarding the Center

The treasure chest represents your greatest potential, the immeasurable gold inside of you. The dragon corresponds to the inner conflict you have in reaching and accessing your greatest potential. In mythology, the dragon guards something that it has no use for, be it a sea of gold coins or a beautiful maiden. In human dynamics, it guards your inner self. In either case, it is guarding it and won't back down unless you confront it.

In the *Power of Myth*, Joseph Campbell talks about "Siegfried's Rhine Journey," an opera by Richard Wagner. In this myth, the hero Siegfried goes into the innermost cave to kill a dragon. After it is slain, the hero drinks its blood to assimilate with it. The hero has conquered the dragon.

Why would the hero drink the blood?

In human dynamics, the dragon represents the force that holds you back. It represents the fears and energy blocks that you put there, once upon a time, to protect yourself. Drinking the blood is symbolic to recognizing, understanding, and accepting what fears and energy blocks are holding you back.

In essence, you made the prison, you hold the key

You need to integrate these experiences, putting them in proper prospective, and then set yourself free, launching yourself toward the success of your vision.

Guiding you toward the defeat of the dragon can be the task of your support system, be it a coach, mentor, or parent. But the final trick, the final killing blow to that dragon, can only be done by you.

Onwards! Towards Achieving Your Goal: Persistence

I know we all want to be seen as smart, intellectual, strong, and without fault. But that can't always be the case.

What it really takes to be successful is not being afraid to learn in the face of scrutiny; having the **persistence** to try, try, and try again; allowing yourself to be adaptable, making mistakes and being what a commentator of *The Botany of Desire* calls, a "public amateur." To be a public amateur means to pursue that which you want and that for which you have a passion, right there in the public's eye. You cannot be afraid of what others will think of you. It means to willfully and bravely be in the moment through the embarrassment and foolish acts.

So don't be afraid to fail or be seen failing, for making mistakes is the key toward mastery. Some of the greatest minds of all time, including Thomas Edison and Albert Einstein, all failed plenty of times before they achieved their successes.

The key here is if you take notes on what was done wrong and learn from these mistakes, it will always make you stronger, stronger than if you took no action at all for fear of humiliation.

Campbell's advice to anyone seeking their way in the world is—to "follow your bliss"—but it may very well feel as if you're making one continuous mistake in trying to find your bliss. Until that moment when it all opens up, places that were once only obstacles, become doors of opportunity. Through all of this, you should not feel as if you're alone, Many others are on their hero's journey as well, and once you meet them you will rejoice!

The most important thing is to be steadfast in your faith that if you are brave and **persistent** in the endeavors of your choosing, you will overcome obstacles. This will no doubt aid in your learning process to achieve mastery in your skill or trade and eventually bring you the success you seek.

As you may be able to see, what I'm writing about here is more than just positive thinking, although positive thinking is a major theme throughout the book. The point I am looking to drive home is more about belief and faith in a bigger sense, and what that belief and faith can bring you. Let's look at these two concepts.

The Importance of Belief and Faith

There is also another theory in Industrial/Organizational Psychology called the Self-Efficacy Theory, which simply states that motivation and performance are determined, in part, by how effective people *believe* they can be. Stephan Krauss describes it this way:

> Self-efficacy is essentially a task specific self-confidence. It's not your level of self-confidence in general, but rather whether you believe you can act in a certain way or carry out a particular course of action. You can ask yourself, 'Can I do task X?' and if the answer you give yourself is 'yes,' then you are high in self-efficacy for that particular task. In study after study, self-efficacy is consistently found to be one of the most powerful predictors of change and success. Relative to those low in self-efficacy, people high in self-efficacy are more likely to...

✓ Set specific challenging goals, and be highly committed to those goals.

✓ Perform better and accomplish more.

✓ Be more proactive, more motivated, and work harder.

✓ Successfully follow through on their New Year's resolutions.

✓ **Persist** vigorously in the face of obstacles, and view setbacks as a source of motivation.

✓ Be successful in tackling problems of depression, anxiety, alcoholism, smoking, and obesity.

✓ Prevent a single lapse from snowballing into a full-blown relapse"

(*Psychological Foundations of Success*, Stephan Krauss, p. 107)

Consistent belief turns into faith, and when that faith turns into action it becomes **persistence**. To finish off this section about persistence and to give you further clarification on how it's all connected here is a section from James 1:1 in the Holy Bible it states:

> Consider it pure joy, my brothers, whenever you face trials of many kinds, because you know the testing of your faith develops perseverance. Perseverance must finish its work so that you may be mature and complete, not lacking anything (NIV).

Defeat your biggest obstacles with faith! Become complete and whole.

Once you realize you lack nothing, you are perfect the way you are. Once you have that belief, the anxious and nervous attitude toward things that keep you down disappears. The beginning of anxiety is the end of faith, and the beginning of true faith is the end of anxiety.

Another reason you should not be in fear or afraid of trials and tribulations in life is because you have the answers within you. With meditation and much practice, you can access the Inner Wisdom Internet. One clear moment within will illuminate the path before you.

When you believe that you have everything in you, you believe in abundance. With this attitude of abundance, you become a mental millionaire; you realize that you are rich, that is; rich with ideas and solutions for the challenges you face. Once this happens you will shift into higher levels of engagement, which will lead to higher levels of production. You have the ability to be creative already within you, it just needs to be activated. Once you understand this principle, then you can really understand the IPEC coaching foundational principle that ***The answers to all questions lie within.***

The Inner Wisdom Internet

When you are engaged to your inner self, your focus is on your inner wisdom when overcoming obstacles. You can unlock your hidden potential, release positive energy, and explore possibilities within yourself to get the job done.

Psychologists (such as Jung) call this *internet* "connecting to the unconscious." You probably have seen or been aware of the iceberg metaphor, which shows ten percent of the iceberg above water and ninety percent under water. That which is above the water represents the conscious mind (the 10%) the rest below represents our unconscious mind (the 90%). Bringing the two together allows for the functioning of 100% of our mental capacity. This is why they say we only use 10% of our minds.

In that 90% of untapped potential lays what Tony Robbins and others call the super-conscious. It's important to note that this section of the unconscious mind includes many, many pieces, one of which is the collective unconscious. It is also safe to say as you uncover more and more of your unconscious, you become more and more conscious of your life and the world around you.

Jung goes as far to say, "Modern man is sick, because he is not whole." With wholeness comes a peaceful union of the conscious and unconscious mind. To really bring this home, let's refer back to Chapter 1 about the nature of consciousness. The activity of consciousness is selective; selection demands direction, and direction requires excluding everything irrelevant. This is bound to make a conscious orientation one-sided. The wholeness Jung discusses is where we bring out our light and darkness together. In fact, this is the only possible solution. In our world of duality, any effort to focus all attention on the light serves to increase the power of darkness. The aim then is to embrace it all. Know the light and know the darkness, their union and combined knowledge will make you strong and luminous.

When you begin to think of large problems such as world peace or ending world hunger, they require the help of a higher power. At a moment's reflection, one can feel the gravity of that burden. These are complex problems that will take linking up to the phenomenal source of all things like the Mystic Law In Buddhism under the Lotus. What I am eluding to here is my conception of "The Inner Wisdom Internet" which you draw from and make requests to. From this phenomenal source, we have access to infinite amounts of information, hope, potential, and solutions. From this source you get the feeling that anything is possible. **This feeling of abundance can be found today, if only we pray and ask for it.**

I also call this an *internet* to respect the diversity of various beliefs. The *internet* I'm referencing here is essentially our spirituality, and no matter how you define it, its existence is the key. This is an approach geared toward global ethics and being a global citizen. As the melting pot of our American culture suggests, diversity is the way to success. Everyone sees things differently, and there is great strength and power in unifying the diversity of people. Just walk down a street in Manhattan, New York. You'll see a diversity of race, culture, and walks of life. This provides us with great problem-solving ability and innovation. The only prerequisite is that we unite personalities and efforts around a central goal.

Now, the specific actions that you take to download or upload to this *internet* and receive its blessings or wisdom are entirely up to you. Many do it by means of prayer, yoga, chanting, meditation, ritual, or simple centering and breathing techniques.

The key is to do whatever feels natural and comfortable for you to induce feelings of calmness and mindfulness as you tap into your own spirituality and higher consciousness. This is important because we all have a center, from which all activity should flow.

In the final analysis, the greatest enemy we have is actually ourselves. Let's refer to the "Dragon Guarding   the

Centre" picture once again (Figure 18), and focus on the **light** emanating from the treasure chest. This is best described by Marianne Williamson:

> Our deepest fear is not that we are inadequate. Our deepest fear is that we are powerful beyond measure. It is our light, not our darkness that most frightens us. We ask ourselves, who am I to be brilliant, gorgeous, talented, and fabulous? Actually, who are you *not* to be? You are a child of God. Playing small does not serve the world. There is nothing enlightened about shrinking so that other people won't feel insecure around you. We are all meant to shine, as children do. We were born to make manifest the glory of God that is within us. It's not just in some of us; it's in everyone. And as we let our own light shine, we unconsciously give other people permission to do the same. As we are liberated from our own fear, our presence automatically liberates others. (*A Return to Love: Reflections on the Principles of A Course in Miracles,* Marianne Williamson)

So the key here is to stand with conviction and speak with your heart and mind, with one intention:

I WILL BE LIGHT!

Now that you have read both Chapter seven
 and Chapter eight.

It's time to take out a journal and write out what helped you
most .

In chapter seven, How could you use Whole Brian
Thinking during your team projects at work?

In Chapter eight,

Is your source of energy more anabolic or catabolic?

Referring to the image "the stress evaluator" Where would
you rate yourself?

Stage Three:
The Return

The philosophy of the empty cup is pretty simple yet profound. A cup's usefulness is when it's empty. If it's already full it cannot contain any more liquid. This is an analogy that represents open-mindedness and closed mindedness.

As the last chapter in this book, we are now covering steps 10-12. We are at the return, aligned with returning your gifts to society and playing your functional role in society. This can be a tricky stage because the special world was fun and you were just starting to get comfortable there. You could become arrogant and prideful thinking highly of yourself because after all you killed the dragon and obtained the reward! Why do you need any one else? You have the reward not them, they should be coming to you! This attitude and "self-talk" can be problematic. Being full of your self can lead to being arrogant and close off to ot5hers, much like having a full cup

It is in this stage where your transformation happens. You have the elixir, reward, insight, vision or invention, which you intend to return with and give to people, but it is anything but a smooth and easy ride back "home."

If life were a smooth highway, we would never be challenged, and we would never develop key life skills. But as you may have learned, life is not a smooth highway, and our journey is full of obstacles and detours. The blessing is that roadblocks standing in our way are essential to our journey to help us grow. These obstacles are needed because it's all part of the evolution from your "current self" to your "new self," where a remarkable transformation occurs.

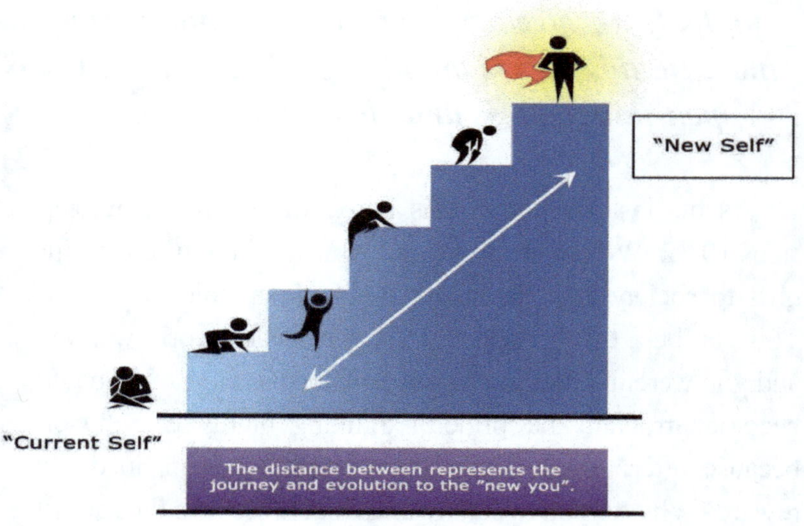

Figure 19

Let's say you win the Megabucks lottery. It's a life changing occurrence. *Bam!* You have an instant influx of cash that you didn't have to earn. One day, you're living paycheck-to-paycheck, and the next day you're a millionaire. The problem is that the road to riches was a smooth superhighway.

There was no transformation process, no challenge, and no indoctrination. You are unprepared for your new position in life. If you are like many lottery winners, you will quickly spend your way back to where you began.

George Leonard gives us these thoughts on this topic:

> This issue isn't just an invention of television. It resonates in the rhetoric about scoring (`I don't care how you win, just win') about effortless learning, instant celebrities, instant millionaires, and the `number one' finger raised in the air when you score just once…..This quick-fix anti-mastery mentality touches almost everything in our lives. Look at modern medicine and pharmacology `fast temporary relief ' is the battle cry, symptoms receive immediate attention; underlying causes remain the shadows. (*Mastery: the Keys to Success and Long-Term Fulfillment,* George Leonard, p. 32–33).

Find your rhythm of success

It is important to find your rhythm of success. Not everybody marches to the beat of the same drummer. To become successful, you must develop your personality, stick to your values, build on your strengths, rely on your instincts, and "learn to love the plateau" as George Leonard writes above. The plateau represents the time where it doesn't seem like you are making progress forward.

Ask anyone who has worked out in a gym for a long time. Over time, you hit a plateau or a wall. It gets more and more difficult to see gains in size and strengths. This can get quite frustrating, but you must stick with it. If you follow this, you will succeed. The last thing you want to do is go to war with yourself or be misaligned, because this will cause incongruences and a lot of tension, stress, and catabolic energy. This will eventually deteriorate you and lead to burn-out, exhaustion, and fatigue.

The transformation from ordinary man to hero

It is also important to recognize the pattern of life outlined in the introduction regarding the "hero's journey." It is the journey of life, to accomplish your dream or vision, and become who you were meant to be. As the "hero's journey" suggests, we need to be encouraged by a mentor and develop our allies. You are the hero. The support system you choose after reading this book is up to you. When we come together as a whole, the whole is much greater than the sum of its parts, and together we are much stronger. We all play a part in the journey of life. Everyone has a unique contribution.

Many writers have based their books on the circular pattern of life. There is a beginning and end that meet each other. Every hero had a mentor to develop and encourage him or her. For this to be possible the person had to be coachable. In essence, this means that one is humble and honest with oneself.

Become humble to achieve greatness

If you need help you should ask for it, and not be stubborn or prideful. Like all great heroes who acknowledged that they didn't know it all, in their humility and courage, they achieved greatness.

The support system you choose will be your guide to achieve greatness. Let's recall the analogy of the empty cup. The philosophy of the empty cup is pretty simple. A cup's usefulness is when it's empty. If it's already full it cannot contain any more liquid. This is an analogy that represents the man who thinks he doesn't need help, and knows everything; his mind is full and cannot contain any more information. In a coaching relationship, your Transformational Coach will presume that you are looking to keep filling your cup to represent the mixing of efforts.

Remember the importance of asking for what you need, *this* will be the beginning of your journey. I am reminded here of what is written in the Scriptures:

"So I say to you: Ask and it will be given to you; seek and you will find; knock and the door will be opened to you" The Holy Bible, (Luke 11:9, NIV)

Short Bio About the Author

This is the story of my own journey to finding my Ideal career. Like most people, I have had a few struggles along the way. The things I will ask you to do on your personal development journey, are the very things I have done myself. I have looked at who I really was and where I wanted to be in life. I continue to examine and resolve blockages that hold me back from my Ideal career success.

I want to share with you some of my first realizations and how I overcame them. I'm a recovering perfectionist – that was number one for me. I finally figured out that if I am always waiting for everything to be perfect, I was going to spend most of my time waiting rather than doing. And guess what? You can't change your life while waiting on the sidelines for the perfect moment to jump into the game, because that perfect moment will never come.

I also knew that I did not want to be a door-to-door salesman long-term. This next part is key. So often, when we decide we don't like a job, we quickly jump to the next "best" job that will provide us a paycheck. I get that. It can be overwhelming to stick it out while you look at all your options and determine what you really want. I decided to do things differently this time. Instead of immediately jumping out of door-to-door sales, I sat back and looked at its components, what interested me, and what I was good at.

I found that I was fascinated by the different people and personalities that I encountered door-to-door, and I began to wonder what made some of them click with me and others show little or no connection at all.

That was the moment that my journey to become a Professional Career Coach began. My fascination with my customer's personalities, led me to become a Myers-Brigg Personality Indicator Practitioner, which led me to IPEC and my certification as a professional career coach.

After going through over 350 hours of coaching, enough hours to become a Master Certified Coach (MCC) according to the International Coaching Federation (ICF) and personally coaching numerous clients, some referred to in my book, I decided that I wanted to write and share my ideas with the masses.

I wrote a book titled Vision In Action. The book and my operating philosophy have a lot to do Industrial and Organizational psychology, positive psychology, and Eastern Philosophy. Also, The psychology of Carl Jung and books like, The Art of War and Samurai Wisdom. One book titled "Ikigai" really gets to the heart of what I do in career coaching. I find the middle point between What you love, What the world needs, what you can be paid for, what you are good at.

Through the ongoing process of examining who I am and where I want to be, I continue to develop knowledge, skills, and experiences that I offer to you as your personal career coach.

185

I could not have written this book alone, I encourage you to explore these resources to expand your knowledge of my process.

<u>Bibliography</u>

Addiss, Stephen, with Stanley Lombardo and Judith Roitman. Introduction by Paula Arai, Editors. *Zen Sourcebook: Traditional Documents from China, Korea, and Japan.* Hackett publishing company Inc. (2008)

Amen, Dr. Daniel G., *Change Your Brain, Change Your Life.* Three Rivers Press; Reprint Edition (1999).

Burleson, Blake W. *Pathways to Integrity.* Paperback CAPT. Center for Applications of Psychological Type (2001).

Buzan, Tony, with Barry Buzan. *The Mind Map Book.* Plume Printing and Penguin Group, (1996).

Campbell, Joseph, Editor. *The Portable Jung.* Penguin Books. (1976). Campbell, Joseph, *Reflections on the Art of Living.* Harper Perennial: First Paperback Printing Edition (1995).

Campbell, Joseph, *Pathways to Bliss*, New World Library. 1st Edition. (2004).

Campbell, Joseph, *The Hero with A Thousand Faces.* New World Library, Third Edition (2008).

Bibliography

Clifton, Donald O. & Paula Nelson, *Soar With Your Strengths*, Dell Publishing (1992)

Csikszentmihalyi, Mihaly, *Flow: The Psychology of Optimal Experience.* Harper Perennial Modern Classics. 1st Edition (2008)

Freidan, Betty. *The Fountain of Age*, New York: Simon and Schuster. (1993)

Giannini, John L. *Compass of the Soul.* Center for Applications of Psychological Type, Inc (2004).

Gladwell, Malcolm. *Outliers.* Back Bay Books/ Little,Brown and company, Paperback (2011).

Hyde, Maggie, and Michael McGuiness. *Introducing Jung.* Totem Books, (1993).

Jackson, Phil. *Sacred Hoops: Spiritual Lessons of a Hardwood Warrior.* New York: Hyperion. (1995).

Jung, C. G. *The Archetypes and the Collective Unconscious.* In R.F.C. Hull (trans.), Collected Works (vol.9i). Princeton, NJ: Princeton University Press. (1959).

Jung, C. G. , and M. Esther Harding. *Psychic Energy, Its Source and its Transformation.* Princeton/Bollingen Paperback Edition, (1973).

Jung. C. G. *Psychological Types: the Collected Works of C. G. Jung.* Princeton University Press; Ninth Printing (1990). **The first translation from German was by H. G. Baynes. Published in 1923 by Kegan Paul, London, and Harcourt, Brace and Co., New York**

Jung, C. G. *The Undiscovered Self.* First Signet Printing (2006).

Keirsey. David. *Please Understand Me II,* Prometheus Nemesis Book Company (1998)

Kolbe, Kathy, *Powered by Instinct.* Monumentus Press; 1 Edition *(2003).*

Kraus, Stephen J., *Psychological Foundations of Success.* Next Level Science (2003).

Laney, Marti Olsen, *The Introvert Advantage, How to Thrive in an Extrovert World.* Workman Publishing Company (2002).

Leonard, George. *Mastery: the Keys to Success and Long-Term Fulfillment. First Plume Printing (1992)*

Lyubomirsky, S;, Sheldon, K M;, and Schkade, D. "Previously Published Works." Pursuing Happiness: The Architecture of Sustainable Change [eScholarship]. UC Riverside, 2005. Fri, 22, March 2013.

"MBTI Basics." *My MBTI personality type.* Myersbriggs, 10th of February 2016

Myers, Isabel Briggs and Peter B. Myers. *Gifts Differing.* Nicholas Brealey Publishing; 2nd edition (1995).

Myers, Isabel Briggs, and Mary H. McCaulley, Naomi L Quenk, Allen Hammer. *MBTI Manual, Third Edition.* (1998).

Pearman, Roger, & Sarah C. Albritton. *I'm Not Crazy, I'm Just Not You.* Davies-Black Publishing, a Division of CPP (1997).

Quenk, Naomi, L. *Was That Really Me?* Davies-Black Publishing, a Division of CPP (2002).

Pollan, Michael. *The Botany of Desire.* Random House Trade Paperbacks; 1st Edition (2002).

Rath, Tom, *Strengths Finder 2.0*, Gallup Press, (2007).

Schneider, Bruce. *Energy Leadership.* Wiley; 1st Edition (2007).

Robison, Jennifer. "Happiness Is Love -- and $75,000." Gallup.com. N.p., 17 Nov. 2011. Web. 16 Feb. 2016

Spector, Paul. *Industrial and Organizational Psychology Textbook, Fifth Edition. John Wiley & Sons, Inc., (2008).*

Suzuki, Shunryu and David Chadwick. *Zen Mind, Beginner's Mind.* Shambhala (2006).

The American Journal of Psychiatry. Vol. 156(2), Feb 1999

Tough, Paul. *How Children Succeed.* Houghton Mifflin Harcourt Publishing Company (2013).

Tzu, Sun. *The Art of War.* Shambhala Publications. Translated by Thomas Cleary (1988). **Sun-Tzu was from 6th Century B.C.**

Tzu. Lau *Tao Te Ching.* Frances Lincoln Limited, (1999)

Vogler, Christopher. *The Writer's Journey.* Sheridan Books, (2007).

Williamson, Marianne. *A Return To Love: Reflections on the Principles of A Course in Miracles*, Harper Collins, (1992).

Internet Sources

http://www.sgi.org/about-us/buddhism-in-daily-life/human-
revolution.html

http://www.myersbriggs.org/my---mbti---personality---
type/mbti---basics/

"Human Revolution." *Buddhism in daily life*. SGI, 10th of
February 2016

FILMS

Documentary Film. *Quantum Activist.* (2009)

Documentary Film. *Happy (2011)*

Documentary Film, *With One Voice (2009)*

Documentary Film, *Finding Joe* (2011)

Bibliography